THE
RAILWAY
AND ITS
PASSENGERS

A Social History

THE
RAILWAY
AND ITS
PASSENGERS
A Social History

DAVID NORMAN SMITH

DAVID & CHARLES
Newton Abbot London North Pomfret (Vt)

For my Mother and Father

Smith, David Norman
  The railway and its passengers: a social
  history.
  1. Great Britain. Railway passenger
  transport services, to 1948
  I. Title
  385'.22'0941

  ISBN 0-7153-8651-4

Phototypeset by Northern Phototypesetting Co Bolton
and printed in Great Britain
by Billings & Sons Ltd Worcester
for David & Charles Publishers plc
Brunel House Newton Abbot Devon

Published in the United States of America
by David & Charles Inc
North Pomfret Vermont 05053 USA

Contents

Special Military Traffic; Railways and Royal Passengers

List of Abbreviations

ELR	East London Railway
GCR	Great Central Railway
GER	Great Eastern Railway
GJR	Grand Junction Railway
GNR	Great Northern Railway
GWR	Great Western Railway
L&BR	London & Birmingham Railway
LBSC	London Brighton & South Coast Railway
LCDR	London Chatham & Dover Railway
L&MR	Liverpool & Manchester Railway
LMS	London Midland & Scottish Railway
LNER	London & North Eastern Railway
LNWR	London & North Western Railway
LSWR	London & South Western Railway
LYR	Lancashire & Yorkshire Railway
MSL	Manchester Sheffield & Lincolnshire Railway
NER	North Eastern Railway
S&CR	Settle & Carlisle Railway
S&DR	Stockton & Darlington Railway
SER	South Eastern Railway

Preface

From the earliest days of steam railways in Britain the relationship between the railway and its passengers raised several crucial questions. Was the market for railway travel simply the creation of the railway or the product of other, more complicated forces in the social and economic structure of Victorian Britain? Did the railway companies actively encourage some types of traffic whilst discouraging others? What sort of services were provided for different classes of passengers? How did the companies react to the growth of commuter traffic or demands for third-class travel and cheap excursion trains? What part did government play in the development of railway travel and how did the companies respond to state interference? How did the companies attempt to promote passenger traffic and sell their services to the public?

Answers to some of these questions may be found if the reader is prepared to consult a wide range of existing, often highly specialised, studies. The standard company histories provide some information on the development of passenger traffic on particular railways, while the more general social and economic histories of transport provide useful chapters on the impact of railways on passenger travel. The work of various social historians has shed light on the railway's role in the rise of the seaside holiday and of the resort towns themselves. Linked to this the railway as urban history and its contribution to the growth of the Victorian city and its suburbs has received detailed attention. Political historians have studied the role of government in railway development. Other aspects of railway passenger operations – notably the development of rolling stock and railway safety – have also been studied.

The aim of this book, therefore, is to bring together into a single volume the various themes in the manifold relationship between the railway and its passengers during the period between 1830 and the nationalisation of Britain's railways in 1947. Little of the content claims to be original since it is essentially a survey and a synthesis of

9

the existing and often very diverse literature in this field. The treatment of the subject, inevitably selective and by no means exhaustive, is thematic. The first chapter outlines the reasons for the rapid growth of railway passenger traffic, its dominant characteristics and the development of railway travel into a 'mass' activity. Chapter two examines the intervention of the state in the relationship between passenger and railway. Subsequent chapters explore the development of various categories of passenger train services – main line, rural, suburban, excursion, special – and the social impact of those services. The final chapter examines the attempts of the railway companies to promote and 'sell' their services to the public, especially in an age of growing competition from other forms of transport.

1
The Impact of Railways on Passenger Travel

Strongly illustrative of the Position, that the Course of True Love is not a Railway

Charles Dickens, *The Pickwick Papers*

The Railway as Passenger Carrier

The promoters of the earliest railways only dimly perceived the possibilities for passenger travel that steam locomotion was to rapidly open up. Those speculators hoping to make a handsome return from the building of the Stockton & Darlington Railway did not expect the carrying of passengers to contribute significantly to their profits. Although a turnpike road existed between the two places passenger traffic was barely sufficient to warrant the running of a single coach three or four times a week and no particular effort was made to encourage passenger traffic on the new railway. The line's main source of revenue was the carriage of coal and even by 1832 an average of only 520 passengers per week made use of the horse-drawn coaches which ran along the railway.[1]

In view of the S&DR's experience the promoters of the Liverpool & Manchester Railway were equally cautious in their assessment of the potential for passenger traffic, preferring instead to emphasise the importance of a 'safe and cheap mode of transit for merchandise.' In Parliament William Huskisson argued the case for the railway on the grounds that the canal monopoly was preventing the expeditious movement of goods, especially cotton. Indeed, the company's prospectus suggested that the railway would offer only 'the fair prospect of a public accommodation which cannot be immediately ascertained.'[2] In the event the L&MR was to prove memorable not only for its application of the technology of the steam engine, but for its success as a passenger carrier. Within a few weeks of the commencement of passenger operations in September 1830 some 800 passengers a day were being carried and such was the demand for travel facilities that the movement of goods did not begin until extra locomotives had been acquired towards the end of year. The number of passengers carried on the L&MR rose from 400,000 in the first year of operation to 475,000 in 1835 and 609,000 in 1838. After the L&MR the managements of the early railways found that revenue from passenger traffic was more important than from goods. Indeed, in aggregate terms, it was not until 1852 that revenue from goods traffic began to exceed that from passengers.[3]

The rapidity with which railway passenger traffic increased was impressive and inspired the contemporary railway 'expert' Dionysius Lardner to remark that 'the brilliant and unexpected results of the business in passenger traffic have not unnaturally dazzled, and engrossed the attention of proprietors, directors and managers.'[4] The total number of passengers carried on Britain's railways increased from 24.5 million in 1842 to nearly 73 million in 1850 and 507 million in 1875. By the early twentieth century the railways were carrying over 1,100 million passengers annually, rising to 1,400 million by the First World War. Although a change in the method of compiling official statistics makes comparison with subsequent years difficult it is estimated that during the inter-war period passenger traffic remained around this level. By 1939, however, passenger traffic on the railways was failing to keep pace with the general increase in passenger journeys by all forms of transport. Between 1920 and 1938 all journeys increased by nearly 50 per cent, but most of the increase was due to the growth in private car ownership and bus services.[5]

In retrospect the reasons for the railway's success as a passenger carrier are not difficult to understand. The railway tapped an existing and expanding market for passenger transport. During the eighteenth century road services had experienced a considerable expansion. Stage and other coach services, often running on the improved roads of the turnpike trusts made a considerable contribution to the speed and volume of passenger travel in the pre-railway age. According to one estimate the passenger mileage covered by coach services between London and 38 provincial centres grew from 67,000 in 1715 to 2,369,000 in 1848.[6] This

Arrival of Christmas Train, Eastern Counties Railway – Drawn by Duncan [*Illustrated London News* 21 December 1850] (by courtesy of the Lancashire Library and by permission of the *Illustrated London News* Picture Library).

rising trend is illustrated by the growth of coach services to the expanding resort of Brighton. In 1731 passengers travelling from London had to endure the hardship of the carrier's waggon, taking a day to complete the journey. By 1811 Brighton boasted 28 coaches running daily between the two centres carrying perhaps 60,000 passengers in the first five months of that year, the average journey time being six hours.[7]

Supplementing road transport services were those provided by coastal vessels. In the days of sail the lower costs of travelling by sea attracted a growing number of passengers, sometimes in preference to competing road (and later rail) services. With the development of steam packet services from about the 1820s, particularly on routes such as London–Margate, Glasgow–Liverpool and Newcastle upon Tyne–London, coastal shipping became the first mass carrier of passengers by steam power.[8]

Meanwhile, inland waterways had been undergoing a continuous process of improvement since the second half of the sixteenth century. The upgrading and extension of river navigation led in this process, the canal 'age' of the second half of the eighteenth century being in many respects the natural culmination of river improvements. Although principally carriers of bulky goods with a low value to weight ratio, rivers and canals did make provision for the carriage of passengers, some remarkably successfully. For example, as late as 1830 the Glasgow, Paisley & Johnstone Canal invested in new, lighter boats capable of speeds of 10 miles per hour and so able to compete with rival coach services. By the mid-1830s five of the principal Scottish canals were carrying over 800,000 passengers annually, while in the industrialising North West of England the Manchester, Bolton & Bury Canal carried over 64,000 passengers during 1833–4.[9]

The expansion of such services suggests that by the later eighteenth and early nineteenth centuries the demand for passenger travel was already 'highly income- and price-elastic'. Expressed another way, any increase in personal income or fall in the cost of travel was likely to result in a rapid increase in the numbers wishing to travel. This, in the words of two modern economic historians, may help to explain 'the paradox of the early railway, promoted for goods carriage but profiting more from the passenger.'[10]

As disposable incomes grew in the nineteenth century so more and more people lower down the social scale than the landed, professional and mercantile classes could take the opportunity to travel. Nevertheless, despite the expansion of the travel market, in absolute terms it remained comparatively small and confined to the more affluent members of society until the coming of the railway. Yet if the railway created new opportunities for travel, initially the main beneficiaries remained those with sufficient time and money to exploit the new transport services. Fares remained relatively high, even on the early railways. Until the availability of cheap fares on the railways the majority of the population, variously described as the 'labouring poor' or 'working classes', could not afford to travel and, in many cases, had no occasion to travel unless in search of work. Until cheaper railway fares the only real inland alternative to walking within the reach of the 'lower orders' was the stage waggon – at 1½d a mile, one quarter of the price of an outside seat on a stage coach.[11] On the whole, therefore, the mass market for travel remained latent, dependent for its realisation upon the percolation downwards through society of the nation's increased wealth and the crucial development of cheaper services by steam railway.

Nevertheless, given the nature and size of the existing and potential market for travel, it is not difficult to see why the railway had its primary impact as a passenger carrier. In terms of the cost, speed and, despite criticisms, comfort of travel the railway offered clear advantages over its rivals. For the 'richer classes' it removed the need for the expensive practice of 'posting'. For the 'middle classes' a journey in a second-class carriage compared favourably with an inside seat in a stage coach, yet fares were generally about half the equivalent coach fare.[12] In addition, by reducing journey times the railway contributed to a further reduction in travel costs since it spared the traveller the additional expense of meals, accommodation and tips en route. Indeed, for many passengers the speed of railway travel was the major inducement to travel; for the 'poorer classes' it was perhaps the only inducement since it was difficult to point to a reduction in costs over travelling on foot.

But the incentive of speed was there for all classes. Despite the considerable reductions in journey times achieved by the stage coaches they were still no match for the railway. The average speed of the early railways was in the region of 28 to 30 miles per hour, providing a reduction in journey times of roughly one third. By 1844 the journey from London to Liverpool which had taken around 21 hours by coach had been cut to just over 8 hours. Journeys between centres closer to London, such as Birmingham and Nottingham, which had taken perhaps half a day by coach, were reduced to a few hours by train. As the efficiency and speed of the railway increased so journey times fell still further. By 1900 the London to Liverpool run could be covered in four and a quarter hours.[13]

There were other attractions which also helped to spread the travel habit. For the aristocracy the train offered convenient movement between their country estates and London for the 'season'. They might even have been encouraged to become regular railway travellers by the displays of deference they received from officials and staff of the railway companies. Preferential treatment was a further incentive. The Great Western Railway, for instance, arranged for some of its trains to stop at a special station at Great Bedwyn for the Marquess of Ailesbury and his heirs. Even lesser mortals were occasionally courted by the companies. The Liverpool & Manchester set an early example in this field providing special trains for the Society of Friends and building stations at Flow Moss and Lamb's Cottage in response to pleas from Chat Moss farmers.[14]

Yet if the majority of railway passengers had to make do without either deference or preferential treatment the habit of railway travel nevertheless soon became accepted and acceptable. While certain medical 'authorities' warned of extensive dangers to health arising from railway travel, especially for those with 'exquisite sensibility of the nervous system' or prone to 'fulness of blood in the head', the vast majority of passengers either ignored or were ignorant of their allegations. In any case serious medical study of the effects of railway travel on the health of both passengers and employees did not begin until the late 1850s – too late to have any major impact on the minds of the travelling public. Even major railway accidents, usually reported in gruesome detail in the press, did little to dent the popularity of travel by train.[15]

The concept of the train journey was soon firmly established and even something of an art in itself. According to A. B. Granville, writer and connoisseur of Europe's spas, there was hardly a 'more dramatic or soul-stirring scene enacted by gas light anywhere in London' than an evening departure from the Euston Square terminus of the London & Birmingham. Granville observed three types of passenger: the 'old hands . . . coolly sauntering, *cigar en bouche*', those who arrived breathless fearful of being 'too late', and those intimidated at the thought of losing their 'property and passage'. The experienced second-class passenger could always be distinguished by their cushions and great coats, for the carriages, although 'closed with glass windows [and] sufficiently snug in winter', had 'not the luxury of cushions, stuffing &c.'[16]

Travellers could also avail themselves of a growing number of guide books drawing attention to station architecture, the geology of the countryside or local history. Reading, window gazing or sleeping were the accepted norms of behaviour, at least in first and second class, and marked a contrast to the lively conversation which had accompanied journeys by stage coach. But if some disliked the oppressive silence of the railway journey, the enforced study of physiognomy, or were fearful of the threat of physical assault in the isolation of the compartment, the majority rapidly took to the new species of conveyance.

The Growth of Third-Class Travel

One of the most significant features of the tremendous increase in the number of people making journeys by rail, especially during the mid-Victorian period, was the rise in third-class traffic. Yet the early companies did little to encourage the 'poorer classes' to avail themselves of the advantages of railway travel. The S&DR did not provide third-class facilities until 1835 and then only because it hoped to dissuade people from the dangerous practice of walking along the course of the railway. The L&MR began operations with a choice of first- or second-class accommodation, third class not being considered until 1840 and not introduced until 1844.[17] The Midland Counties Railway was typical of many early companies. Although it carried third-class passengers the carriages were no more than open boxes without seats. Carrying sixty passengers it was assumed that 'no one will go in it who can afford to go in others . . . the passengers all stand, they are taken as the pigs are.'[18] The Great Western provided carriages of 'an inferior description at very

Third-class passengers enduring carriages described as 'a species of shower bath', *Illustrated London News* 7 December 1844 (by courtesy of the Lancashire Library Preston District and by permission of the *Illustrated London News* Picture Library).

low speeds' for its third-class patrons and, like the London & South Western and London & Birmingham, 'combined them with cattle, horses and empty wagons.'[19]

Class snobbery no doubt played a part in producing such discrimination. C. A. Saunders, Secretary of the GWR, claimed on several occasions during the 1840s that the behaviour of third-class passengers caused offence to other classes of passengers – a view which presumably explains his company's determination to segregate the classes both on trains and stations. The belief that the 'lower orders' would annoy, even drive away, higher class patrons, or simply vandalise railway property was a recurring theme in railway history. In 1883, for example, the Chairman of the NER complained that when curtains had been provided in third-class carriages the passengers had 'cut them off, and probably used them as pocket-handkerchiefs.'[20]

Class prejudice certainly existed, but it is doubtful if it was the only influence on railway policy. Underlying the business strategies of most companies were more hard-headed, commercial considerations. Many of the early main line companies believed that a select, high-class business was the most profitable. They feared that third-class trains would increase the numbers travelling but, because of the lower fares, not necessarily their revenue. In the case of two companies – the Leeds & Selby and the Manchester, Bolton & Bury – it was found that increasing the fares caused the number of passengers to decline, but revenue to increase.[21]

Under these circumstances it was hardly surprising that the development of travel facilities for those on 'daily wages' was retarded. Yet the growth of third-class traffic during the second half of the nineteenth century was spectacular. In 1846 third-class passengers still comprised less than half the total of all passengers carried and contributed only 20 per cent of total revenue. By 1870 the proportion of passengers travelling third class had increased to 65 per cent, contributing 44 per cent of total revenue. The decisive shift in the importance of the third-class passenger occurred between 1850 and 1865. According to the calculations of one historian, third-class receipts on the London & North Western Railway increased from 33 to 45 per cent of total receipts during this period; on the GWR the rise was from 27 to 45 per cent; on the

London Brighton & South Coast 43 to 53 per cent; on the South Eastern Railway 41 to 59 per cent; on the Lancashire & Yorkshire Railway 59 to 65 per cent; and on the LSWR 28 to 41 per cent.[22] As the Royal Commission on Railways of 1867 acknowledged, the rapid increase in all passenger traffic during this period was fuelled predominantly by the growth of third-class traffic. By 1890 this trend had become even more marked. Boosted by the abolition of second class on many railways, the proportion of passengers travelling third class had increased to nearly 96 per cent.

The standard explanation for the growing importance of the third-class passenger to the railways during the mid-Victorian period emphasises the passing of Gladstone's Railway Act of 1844. Section six of the Act obliged all passenger railway companies to run at least one train each week day at a maximum fare of one penny per mile. That the Act was valuable in demonstrating the demand for better travelling facilities for third-class passengers cannot be disputed. However, resistance from several companies to the extension of 'parliamentary trains' beyond the statutory minimum did not disappear overnight, even if some had begun to look more favourably upon the commercial possibilities of third-class travel.[23] Moreover, travel at a penny per mile under the 1844 Act, though a step in the right direction, remained beyond the purses of many working-class households. Further reductions in fares were essential if third-class travel on a daily basis was to become a reality. Thus, cheap fares for workmen, introduced as a response to statutory provisions in individual railway Acts, under the terms of the Cheap Trains Act of 1883, or simply for commercial reasons did much to increase regular third-class travel after the 1860s.

The provision of other cheap fares, notably on excursion trains, was also to play an important role in the popularity of the travel habit. Commercial considerations rather than statutory requirements were paramount in explaining the railway companies' expansion of excursions. By the 1840s and 1850s the excursion train had already become an accepted part of railway operations. During the second half of the century they proliferated both in number and choice of destinations. Although not the sole preserve of the third- or working-class passenger, the railway excursion rapidly became a popular institution, linking the railway indelibly with passengers' leisure activities of all kinds, but above all with day trips to the countryside or seaside.

As third-class travel grew in importance the railway companies also began to provide better facilities for the third-class passenger on 'ordinary' train services. This policy was not just the outcome of a growing awareness of the commercial importance of third class; increasing competition between several companies led to notable attempts during the last few decades of the century to attract third-class passengers by providing greater comfort and quicker services. The leader was the Midland Railway with the provision of penny a mile services on some fast trains to London in 1868 (extended to all Midland trains in 1872), and the simultaneous abolition of all second-class accommodation and improvement of standards of accommodation in third class in 1874.[24] Similar policies introduced by rival companies, not always in response to the Midland Railway, ensured that by the end of the nineteenth century the standard of accommodation and service on many third-class trains had improved immeasurably and the gap between first and third reduced. Although standards on some railways and most local trains remained rudimentary, on express and long-distance trains at least third-class passengers were able to benefit from what one historian has termed a decisive shift 'from the Middle Ages of railway travel into the beginnings of the modern world.'[25]

In another sense too the acceptance of the legitimate claim of the third-class passenger for decent standards of accommodation at reasonable fares and speeds marked a further and more symbolic step into the modern world. The railway had gone some way towards fulfilling the idealistic aspirations of those intellectuals who viewed the railway as a vehicle for ushering in an age of greater equality and freedom. As one French commentator observed:

> It is the same convey, the same power that carries the great and the small, the rich and the poor; thus the railroads most generally provide a continuous lesson in equality and fraternity.[26]

It was an exaggeration. Inequality certainly did not disappear with the construction and prolonged operation of the railway either in Britain or Europe, while the train could just as easily, and with horrific results, be turned to the needs of war between nations as travel in the cause of fraternity. Moreover, there were many who

A DANGEROUS CHARACTER

Policeman Sibthorpe, "Come, it's high time you were taken to the House; you've done quite mischief enough." (Reproduced by permission of *Punch* and by courtesy of the Lancashire Library Blackburn district)

viewed the potential for the 'mass movement' of the lower orders by railway train as undesirable and a potential threat to public order. It was not, after all, the fear of the physical danger of railway travel that provoked Lord de Mowbray's opposition to railways in Disraeli's novel *Sybil*: 'Equality, Lady Marney, equality is not our metier. If we nobles do not make a stand against the levelling spirit of the age, I am at a loss to know who will fight the battle. You may depend upon it these railroads are very dangerous things.'[27]

Yet if some early Victorians were mortified by the thought of travel for the masses, by the end of the century the concept was taken for granted. In this the pioneering contribution of the railway to the twentieth century revolution in personal mobility and communications was immense. The jet aeroplane and the motor vehicle; 'mass' leisure and the package tour; suburban life and the commuter: these characteristic features of modern industrial society are essentially offshoots of important changes which began in an earlier age with the building of the steam railway. The origins of these changes and the wider relationship between the railway, its passengers and society are explored in the following chapters.

2
Government and the Railway Passenger

M.P.'s may love railways and golden store;
But they should do honour and justice more.

Moore Travestie[1]

Until nationalisation in 1947 the construction and operation of railways in Britain was the responsibility of private enterprise. Planned and built by private companies, using the not inconsiderable supplies of private capital available both locally and nationally the railway network which had emerged by the 1850s owed little to rational planning or national interests. The guiding principle was anticipated profit and securing the maximum return on capital invested.

In theory it was the task of parliament to decide between rival railway projects and impose some restraint on the forces of competitive free enterprise. Parliament had long been interested in trade and transport matters – inquiring into the alleged poor state of the roads, passing private Acts facilitating the creation of turnpike trusts, the improvement of navigations or the building of canals. By inserting clauses into private Acts stipulating the amount of capital to be raised and the charges or tolls for the use of the road or waterway, parliament also attempted to protect the public interest against the dangers of financial malpractice and monopoly.

Since railways followed in this tradition and were built under powers contained in private Acts of parliament, the procedures involved gave committees of both Houses the opportunity to screen and amend each new railway project. In this sense the railway companies, since they derived their powers from private Acts, were 'creatures of Parliament'.[2] However, parliamentary procedures were time consuming, cumbersome and frequently irrational. In practice, the role of the state in the planning and construction of railways was minimal: 'The lines promising the most ample returns', lamented the Select Committee on Railway Acts

Enactments in 1846, 'were, as a matter of course, first selected by companies; but the best mode of communicating the benefit of railways to the kingdom ... as a whole, was only incidentally considered by committees in deciding between rival projects.'[3]

In entrusting the development of such a vital national asset to the competition and speculation of private enterprise British practice differed sharply from several other European states. The Belgian government, for example, involved itself in both the planning and construction of railways in an attempt to gain better access to European markets and thereby compete more effectively with their commercial rivals in the Netherlands. The French government saw railways as important public works, supplying the necessary land and infrastructure, before leasing the railways to private operating companies. Government influence was also significant in German railway building. Since Germany as a unified nation did not exist until 1870 the railway became an important agent in the spread of government control over the various regions and the breaking down of social, economic and cultural barriers to effective unification.[4]

Such strategic and political considerations were not entirely absent in Britain. The ability of the railways to move troops rapidly to internal trouble spots, especially during the Chartist disturbances, was soon recognised.[5] The defence implications of the railways were also evident. In 1846 the Gauge Commissioners noted that the continued existence of Brunel's broad gauge of 7ft and the narrow (later standard) gauge of 4ft 8½in could in the event of invasion 'produce both delay and confusion [and] expose the country to serious danger.'[6]

However, such considerations were never sufficiently pressing to warrant more positive intervention by the British state. Nevertheless, as attention turned from construction towards the development of railway passenger services, it became clear that there were several areas of conflict between the interests of companies and travelling public. As early as 1839 a House of Commons Select Committee on Railways noted that 'cases have already arisen in which the interests of private [railway] Companies and of the Public have been found to be opposed to each other.'[7] Later, in 1872, another Select Committee recorded its views on the nature of the conflict:

Self-interest . . . still is and will continue to be the leading motive of railway companies. . . . It is . . . to the interest of the companies to make as large a profit with as little outlay as possible; it is, therefore to their interests to carry one passenger . . . for a shilling, rather than to carry two passengers . . . for sixpence each, whilst the converse is clearly to the interest of the public.[8]

While the railways remained in the hands of private companies the government was torn between demands from the public for greater state control and regulation of the railways and the demands of the industry for freedom from state interference. Although state policy was rarely formulated with any consistency or clarity, over time the relationship between the railway and its passengers was to be influenced in three crucial areas: railway safety, the cost of railway travel, and state control of the process of company amalgamation.

The Government and Railway Safety

The question of public safety provided arguably the most important reason for state intervention in the railway industry. The operation of early railways was attended by all manner of risks to life and limb. The unreliability of engines caused frequent breakdowns and late running, the dangers of collision on such occasions exacerbated by the potentially lethal practice of despatching light engines, wrong line, to find 'missing' trains. At the other extreme it was not unknown for special trains to turn up unexpectedly. On the GWR, for instance, an experimental train conducted by the railway 'expert' Dionysius Lardner was involved in two accidents in as many months. The hazards of early railway operation were heightened by rudimentary signalling, particularly the lack of uniformity between companies. While drivers remained confined to their own stretch of line the risks from the diversity of systems were minimised. However, the growth of through traffic in the 1850s and 1860s lent some urgency to the need for standardisation.[9]

Surprisingly the number of accidents which could be directly attributed to inherently unsafe working practices in the early years was small. But even by the 1860s one of the leading railway guides of the day felt it necessary to advise railway passengers to leave the train in the event of an 'absolute stoppage', while 'in cases where the

26

carriages are felt to be overturning [they must] jump from the upper side as the carriages go over.' It was surely only the most prescient passenger who would be able to anticipate a 'concussion' (collision) and 'without hesitation, throw himself on the floor of the carriage.'[10]

Travelling in compartments isolated from the rest of the carriage and the absence, until relatively late in the century, of a reliable mechanical means of communicating with the train crew also raised the threat of physical assault from fellow passengers. For example, an early passenger who survived a frenzied attack during a journey from Liverpool to Chester later described how the assailant grabbed his hand then, having 'bit my thumb off clean to the bone . . . he held it in his mouth, pushed his head through the glass, spat the thumb into his hand and flung it through the window.'[11] It is difficult to visualise this and other unfortunate victims of assault adopting the advice of the same railway guide that in the event of accidents or emergencies the passengers should attempt to catch the attention of the guard by 'tying a coloured handkerchief to the end of a stick and holding it out as far beyond the carriage as possible.'[12]

Although the dangers of accidents and attack were frequently exaggerated by the popular press, they nevertheless raised several important questions. Could the companies be relied upon to conduct their operations in the safest possible manner? Would voluntary action and agreement be sufficient to ensure investment in the latest safety devices and the standardisation of working practices? If not then should the state intervene and what form should that intervention take? Although state intervention in the industry increased steadily during the nineteenth century no clear or consistent railway policy was to emerge. In matters of railway safety it was assumed that responsibility for the safe working of each railway should rest with the management of the companies concerned. Nevertheless, from 1840 onwards intervention gradually increased as the state exhorted and, in the case of major safety devices, eventually compelled the companies to improve railway safety.

The Regulation of Railways Act of 1840 gave to the Board of Trade powers to inspect new railway lines before they were opened to the public. Under a second Act of 1842 the Board was given further powers to postpone the opening of a line if it was considered dangerous 'by reason of the incompleteness of the works or permanent way, or the insufficiency of the establishment for working such railway.'[13] For lines opened to the public the Board henceforth relied heavily on the power of inspection and the publication of reports to cajole rather than coerce the companies into improving safety. At times, notably during the 1860s, the Board attempted to use public opinion to bring pressure to bear on the companies. Captain H. W. Tyler, head of the Railway Department of the Board of Trade, believed strongly that government coercion would remove responsibility from those involved in the day to day operation of the railways. He was also convinced that the pressure of public opinion was instrumental to voluntary progress.[14]

However, during the late 1860s and early 1870s demands for more direct government intervention grew more vociferous. The impetus came from the higher rate of fatal accidents during these years caused principally by higher speeds and more intensive working. Nevertheless, the first breach in the principle of voluntarism did little to promote the cause of government supervision. In 1868 it was made compulsory for every passenger train, travelling at more than 20 miles per hour, to have 'an efficient means of communication between the passengers and the servants of the company.'[15] Experience with the prescribed communication cord system proved unsatisfactory and the device was withdrawn from use several years later.

Mandatory legislation with regard to other major safety devices, especially in the areas of signalling and braking, remained a long way off. A Select Committee appointed to investigate railway accidents in 1857 had already reported in favour of the telegraphic block system. This was superior to the traditional time interval system since it kept a physical space or 'absolute block' between trains. Two further aids to fail-safe working were also being developed at this time. The first, the interlocking of points and signals, made it impossible for a signalman to inadvertently set up a conflicting route for trains. The second, the automatic continuous brake, ensured the operation of the brakes in the event of a train dividing.

During the 1870s and 1880s the introduction of these devices proceeded by voluntary action on the part of the companies.

Meanwhile the Board of Trade began to find it increasingly difficult to rely on the good will of the companies. Early in 1872 the President of the Board of Trade decisively rejected a call from a questioner in the House of Lords for compulsion in the matter of safety, retorting that the companies were already investing considerable sums in the block and interlocking systems and required more time. Nevertheless by the end of that year the Board found it necessary to issue a circular to the companies complaining that safety devices were being introduced too slowly.[16] The attitude of some railway directors also did little to commend the voluntary principle to the Board. Lord Houghton of the LYR exemplified the inveterate opposition to compulsion, arguing in the Lords that the public 'were well satisfied to run a small risk of accident for the great convenience of frequency and celerity.'[17]

It was against this background that the Royal Commission on Railway Accidents in 1877 recommended granting to the Board of Trade powers to enforce the adoption of the block and interlocking systems.[18] The Commission had also investigated the subject of train brakes. During 1875 several companies took part in a series of brake tests on the Midland Railway near Newark. Although the results were inconclusive they persuaded the Commission that the time had come to recommend that all trains should have sufficient brake power to bring them to a halt within 500 yards.[19] However, with several competing systems available and continued technical development, the Commission was not inclined to recommend any particular system. The experience of the LNWR illustrated the difficulties. Beginning with the Clark and Webb chain brake system, which had the disadvantage of 'fetching the passengers off their seats in a manner most trying to their nerves', the company had also experimented with the continuous vacuum brake and later the automatic vacuum brake. Other companies such as the Midland and North Eastern opted for the competing Westinghouse air brake, but found that this too was also subject to modification and improvement.[20]

Under these circumstances the case for mandatory legislation on brakes was difficult to make out. But the same excuse could not be made for the failure to implement the recommendations of the Commission on the block and interlocking systems. It is true that voluntary progress by the companies was maintained. Between

29

1873 and 1889 the percentage of double-tracked passenger lines in the U.K. operated on the absolute block system increased from 42 to 95, while over the same period the proportion of locations equipped with interlocking rose from 39 to 91 per cent.[21] Nevertheless, behind the scenes the companies exerted a considerable restraining influence and were able to exploit both the lack of unanimity on the best safety systems and the fact that the government was invariably faced by a welter of other administrative business.[22]

It was to take the horrific accident at Armagh in 1889 to jolt Parliament into action. This accident, involving the runaway of part of a Sunday School excursion and its collision with a following train, revealed with tragic results what could happen in the absence of the block system and proper continuous brakes. In the collision 78 passengers, including 22 children, were killed and 260 seriously injured. The shock of the disaster resulted in the passing of the Regulation of Railways Act of 1889 which made the introduction of continuous automatic brakes, the absolute block system and the interlocking of points and signals compulsory on all British railways.[23]

Despite its significance the legislation of 1889 represented not so much the culmination of nineteenth century government policy with regard to railway safety, but an exception to it. Although the principal safety devices were now compulsory, government continued to rely on the long process of inspection, report and persuasion in other areas of safer railway working. In the twentieth century the emphasis was less upon the primary causes of accidents than the tragic effects, particularly fires and the telescoping of carriages, which could be much more destructive of life than the initial collision or derailment. In addition the failure of the human element in the operation of intrinsically safe systems of working came under increasing scrutiny.

The discipline and conscientiousness of railway workers had been a constant theme since the earliest days of railway operation. Throughout the nineteenth century railway workers paid for the stability of their job and the regularity of income it provided in terms of long hours of work, poor working conditions and coercive systems of managerial control. From 1840 the companies' internal disciplinary codes were reinforced by government legislation.

Under the Railway Acts of 1840 and 1842 it was established that railway workers accused of misconduct or negligence might be tried by justices of the peace and subject to fine or imprisonment. Henceforth, the rules of several companies stated clearly that any breach of the rules could lead to prosecution under the terms of this legislation.[24] The intention was clear, as *Herapath's Railway Journal* was quick to recognise: 'The dread of severe punishment will be the only way to keep men of the class of those employed on railways in order.'[25]

The fear of punishment and dismissal must have had a sobering effect on many railwaymen. But it is difficult to reconcile the companies' need for a disciplined workforce with their insistence that the introduction of safety devices would actually reduce the vigilance of staff and thereby increase the chance of accidents. This was a spurious argument, belied by the fact that it was not passengers but railwaymen themselves who were most at risk from accidents. In the mid 1870s, for example, over 700 railwaymen were killed and some 3,500 injured at work each year. Moreover, although the companies had been legally obliged since Lord Campbell's Act of 1846 to pay compensation to passengers killed or injured in railway accidents, they were under no such obligation to their own employees.

Safety at work, adversely affected by excessive hours and poor working conditions, was one of the principal concerns of the first permanent trade union for railwaymen, the Amalgamated Society of Railway Servants formed in 1871. Yet despite pressure from the railwaymen for a reduction in working hours and mounting evidence from the Board of Trade that long hours were a major contributory cause of accidents, it was not until 1893 that a Select Committee on Railway Servants Hours of Work reported that the needs of public safety justified the statutory regulation of hours of work.[26] The resulting Railway Servants (Hours of Labour) Act of the same year allowed the Board of Trade to impose hours of work which it deemed reasonable. Subsequent Acts in 1897 and 1900 extended the Board's powers and also made the companies liable to pay compensation determined by the courts to workmen injured on duty.

Although opinions vary on the impact of this legislation it was a step in the right direction. Nevertheless, it was not until just prior to the First World War, in an atmosphere of deteriorating industrial relations on the railways, that hours of work in the industry were brought down to levels comparable to other sectors. Moreover, although the government was now heavily involved in the regulation of railway safety this did not remove the ultimate responsibility for railway accidents. This remained with the signalmen, drivers, firemen, guards and other staff whose mistakes and misinterpretations would be critically examined in the event of accidents.[27]

The Government and Railway Fares

The government was to exert an earlier, if somewhat contradictory, influence over railway fares. From 1832 a passenger duty was payable by the railway companies at the rate of a halfpenny per mile, payable on every four passengers conveyed (changed in 1842 to a duty of five per cent upon gross passenger receipts). Coaching concerns had long been subject to a duty on their vehicles irrespective of the density of their occupancy. It would have been regarded as grossly unfair if occupied seats on passenger trains had been left completely untaxed. The imposition of the passenger duty added to the cost of railway travel and did little to encourage the development of third-class passenger traffic. However, in subsequent legislation designed to reduce the cost of travelling and provide minimum standards of accommodation, government became involved in extending the appeal of railway travel to poorer sections of society. In practice the provision of 'cheap trains' was linked to the question of the passenger duty.

Gladstone's Railway Act of 1844 obliged the companies to run at least one train a day in each direction, stopping at all stations, at a minimum speed of 12 miles per hour. The carriages were to be provided with seats and protected from the weather. The fare for these services – 'parliamentary trains' as they were dubbed – was not to exceed one penny for every mile travelled. In return the railway companies were exempted from the payment of passenger duty on the trains concerned.[28]

The inclusion of these clauses made Gladstone's Act arguably 'the earliest and perhaps the most dramatic interference with railway companies in the conduct of their business.'[29] Yet as one recent railway historian has noted the cheap train provisions of the Act are sometimes misunderstood. Compared to the wages of those who were expected to benefit from the legislation, penny-a-mile travel was by no means 'cheap'. What made the Act really useful to third-class passengers was the stipulation that they were also entitled to carry with them 56lbs of luggage free of charge. This allowance was a useful concession to workers who found it necessary to move in search of work and reveals one of the principal motivations behind the Act, improving labour supply.[30] It also contributed to some additional discomfort in third-class compartments, in the words of one railway guide dooming the unwary passenger to 'semi-suffocation, and to partial extinction of vision, and total deprivation of motive power [caused] by several large bundles, boxes, or baskets, which every other passenger insists upon carrying.'[31]

The powers given to the Board of Trade under Gladstone's Act were exercised with relish. The Board's Railway Department rigorously investigated fares per mile, average speeds, the timing of parliamentary trains and even set standards of passenger accommodation in advance of the statutory minimum.[32] As a result the open carriage was virtually eliminated from all but excursion services by the end of the 1840s. As replacements the companies built a variety of enclosed, though still primitive, vehicles. An LSWR design of the period was typical. Comprising three compartments with accommodation for thirty passengers, it had curtains to keep out the cold or the dust according to the season but no lighting. Although an improvement on what had gone before, third-class penny-a-mile travel remained something of an endurance test, the accommodation cramped and unyielding, the ventilation inadequate and, in some carriage designs, not even the possibility of a view of the passing countryside to relieve the monotony.

Despite the rigours of mid-Victorian third-class travel the numbers travelling increased enormously during this period. With many companies beginning to run more trains with third-class accommodation than the statutory minimum it became customary for the Board of Trade to exempt certain 'ordinary' trains from passenger duty. Indeed, the companies were encouraged to seek such exemption by the discretionary powers contained in the 1844

Act. The Board of Trade could dispense with any of the conditions relating to parliamentary trains, with the exception of the penny-a-mile provision, 'in consideration of such other arrangements, either in regard to speed, covering from the weather, seats or other particulars . . . more beneficial and convenient for the passengers.[33] Henceforth, the development of third-class travel on most lines was facilitated by the willingness of the Board to remit the duty, especially on trains which did not stop at all stations.[34]

However, during the 1860s the Board's activities began to attract the interest of another branch of government with very different priorities, the Inland Revenue. The amount yielded by the passenger duty had increased considerably, from £153,000 in 1842 to £500,000 in 1868.[35] As the commercial significance of third-class traffic to the companies grew so the loss of a potentially large amount of duty provoked successive attempts to define more rigorously which trains were and which were not entitled to remittance of duty. This culminated in a test case involving the North London Railway in 1874 which confirmed that the Board of Trade had no power to dispense with the once important, but now tedious, condition that trains should stop at every station to qualify for remittance.[36]

By the 1870s many railway companies had decided that the continued imposition of the passenger duty placed an unfair burden on the industry's development. To mobilise opposition to the duty and press for its abolition the companies formed the Passenger Duty Repeal Association in 1874. Three years later another body, the Travelling Tax Abolition Committee, joined in the campaign against the duty. Led and supported by individuals from the labour movement, the Committee agitated for improvements in railway facilities for working-class passengers including the unconditional abolition of the duty.[37] However, it was unlikely that the government would bow to pressure from either the industry or a section of its consumers without securing from the railway companies some concessions in return. As in 1844, the issue of the passenger duty became enmeshed in the wider issue of cheaper railway fares.

Arrival of the Workmen's Penny Train at the Victoria Station [*Illustrated London News* 22 April 1865]. The provision of such services for the 'exclusive accommodation of artisans, mechanics, and daily labourers, both male and female' was, according to the *ILN*, 'an interesting experiment in social economics' (by courtesy of the Lancashire Library Preston District and by permission of the *Illustrated London News* Picture Library).

Workmen's Trains and the Cheap Trains Act, 1883

The resurgence of interest in the provision of cheap train services was linked to the emergence of social reform, especially the urban housing problem, as a major political issue during the 1870s and 1880s. The continued existence of intolerable conditions in inner-city districts – areas of poor, often insanitary, working-class housing – was one of the most serious social problems of the period. Overcrowding and the related problem of public health was aggravated by natural increases in city populations and the loss of working-class housing due to commercial and industrial development, including the building of railways themselves. In London, for example, it is estimated that between 1853 and 1885 some 56,000 people were evicted prior to the demolition of their homes by railway construction.[38]

The solution sought by many city authorities was the dispersal of the working classes from the crowded and unhealthy inner districts to areas of new housing further out. But the success of such policies required adequate and sufficiently inexpensive transit facilities for the daily journey from suburban terrace to work. Clearly the railways could play an important part in the provision of such services. The problem was that existing fare levels, including penny-a-mile services, were far too expensive for most workmen to contemplate a daily return journey by train. Having contributed to the urban housing problem it seemed logical that the railways should be required to run special workmen's trains at reduced fares to compensate.[39]

To a limited extent this was already being done in London where several companies with lines through the inner districts ran workmen's trains as specified in their enabling Acts. But by the early 1880s reports from both the Select Committee on Artisans' and Labourers' Dwellings and the Railway Department of the Board of Trade confirmed complaints that workmen's train services were inadequate, often overcrowded and in some cases inconveniently timed.

These conclusions offered the President of the Board of Trade, the radical Liberal Joseph Chamberlain, an opportunity to intervene. The result was the Cheap Trains Act of 1883 which linked a long overdue revision in the passenger duty with attempts to increase and improve the provision of cheap workmen's trains. Under the Act the old stipulation that a train must stop at every station in order to qualify for exemption from duty was abolished by the simple expedient of repealing the duty on any train with fares not exceeding one penny a mile.[40] Henceforth, penny-a-mile fares on express as well as slow trains were exempted. In return the companies were obliged to run more workmen's trains at reduced fares. No minimum standards were laid down, but if the Board of Trade believed the service inadequate or fares unreasonable, it could deprive the company of exemption from duty on all its penny-a-mile services.[41]

On the whole the companies acquiesced in the measure even though it was a clear example of state interference in their 'commercial' relationship with the passenger. Some companies, notably those controlled by the maverick railway chairman and director Sir Edward Watkin, were hostile to the new Act. But a campaign by the Association of Railway Shareholders against the Act, backed and orchestrated by Watkin's companies, was dismissed by one of the leading railway journals as 'mere claptrap and verbiage.'[42] From the passenger's perspective the Act was certainly significant. It relieved the third-class passenger from the burden of paying duty on all but the slowest of services. At the same time it encouraged the growth of cheaper surburban services. Of course, workmen's trains had not originated with the 1883 Act, but it facilitated a considerable expansion in their number and scope over the next thirty years or so.

However, in the longer term the intervention of the state to secure cheaper travelling facilities for third-class passengers became superfluous. After the First World War the concept of cheap fares for workmen and others was gradually extended voluntarily by the companies for the wholly commercial reason of competing with road transport services. By 1938 over 85 per cent of all railway passenger receipts came from reduced fares (excluding workmen's and season tickets).[43] Under these circumstances the continued imposition of passenger duty on some classes of travel had become anachronistic and the duty was finally abolished on all services by the Finance Act of 1929.

The Government and Railway Monopoly

The regulation of the railway's monopolistic tendencies was probably the most intractable problem facing the state in its dealings with the industry. As with the problems of safety and fares government policy was neither clear nor consistent. Initially it was assumed that railway companies would operate like the canals, opening their lines to competing 'carriers' who would operate trains on payment of the appropriate toll. It was for this reason that the private Acts facilitating railway construction contained clauses stipulating maximum tolls. In this sense railways had been welcomed because they offered the prospect of increasing rather than diminishing competition.

Experience rapidly demonstrated this to be a naive conception of the nature of railways. As we have seen, safety considerations alone dictated that 'upon every Railway there should be one system of management, under one superintending authority, which should have the power of making and enforcing all regulations necessary for the protection of passengers.'[44] In short, the railway companies acted as both owners and operators of the line acquiring a monopoly of traffic as a result. The speed with which the railways eliminated the competition for passenger traffic from road, canal and, to a lesser extent, coastal shipping services heightened fears of monopoly. As the Select Committee on Railways of 1844 observed:

> the very complaint of Monopoly which is urged against Railway Companies, is an indication and a measure of the increased accommodation of the Traffic of the Country which they have afforded, inasmuch as it has not been so much by force of Statutory Enactments granting to them special privileges, as by superior cheapness, security, and rapidity of Travelling, that their command of the intercourse of the districts has been acquired.[45]

Yet it was not the 'natural superiority' of the railways over other forms of travel, but the tendency towards company amalgamation which raised the most serious issues of public policy. The early railways were planned and constructed independently with little thought for the emergence of a 'system'. Their conversion into a national network occurred by a haphazard process of 'amalgamations, consolidation, or fusion.'[46] From the mid-1840s company amalgamations began to be conceived on a much grander scale, raising the possibility of district or regional monopolies. However, virtually every committee or commission which studied the problem – four major enquiries in 1846, 1852–3, 1872 and 1911 – differed in its opinion on the desirability or otherwise of amalgamation.

One of the main reasons for the confusion was that the effects of amalgamation on railway users were far from clear. For most of the nineteenth century sections of the trading community were consistently dissatisfied with freight rates and handling charges and were never slow to accuse certain companies of abusing their monopoly. On the other hand, the railway passenger probably had more to gain from amalgamation than the freight customer. Longer through journeys, better connections and the survival of unprofitable branch lines were arguably the benefits of company concentration. Indeed, it was not always certain that the elimination of competition would result in higher fares for passengers. 'The benefits arising from [amalgamation]', argued the Select Committee on Railway Amalgamation in 1846, 'are undisputable. It enables companies to conduct their operations with less expense and consequently with diminished charges to the Public.'[47] But this was a point on which railway leaders were themselves often in disagreement. In 1872, for example, the General Manager of the NER assured a Select Committee that amalgamations had produced reductions in fares, evidence contradicted by Edward Watkin who suggested that it was increased competition on certain routes which had produced fare reductions.[48]

It was easy to issue platitudes about the dangers of monopoly, but more difficult to establish consistent guidelines on amalgamation, particularly when it could not be clearly demonstrated that it was harmful to the public interest. Although on occasions government acted to block proposals to form giant companies – such as the attempts to merge the LNWR, LSWR and LBSC in 1852–3, and LYR and LNWR in 1872, or the GCR, GNR and GER in 1909 – on the whole concentration in the industry went unchecked and the initiative remained firmly located in railway boardrooms. By 1914 some 1,100 formerly independent companies had been reduced to 100 of which 15 controlled 84 per cent of total railway mileage.[49]

RAILWAY AMALGAMATION – A PLEASANT STATE OF THINGS

Passenger. 'What's the Matter Guard?'
Guard (with presence of Mind). 'Oh, nothing particular, Sir. Weve only run into an Excursion Train!'
Passenger. 'But, Good Gracious! There's a train just behind us, isn't there?'
Guard. 'Yes, Sir!' But a boy has gone down the line with a Signal; and it's very likely they'll see it!'

'Despite the passage of many regulative Acts and the establishment of the Railway and Canal Commission, there had been no legislation generally formulating the policy of Parliament towards combination among railway companies.'[50] Arguably this did not come until after the First World War. The Railways Act of 1921 which amalgamated Britain's railways into four groups – the London, Midland & Scottish, Great Western, London & North Eastern and Southern – can be interpreted as a belated attempt by government to direct for the first time a tendency over which it had previously exercised very little control.

Competition and Monopoly?: The Grouping to Nationalisation

The Railways Act of 1921 emerged out of the debate on the future ownership and structure of the railways following government control during the First World War. The war had caused a serious run-down in track and rolling stock due to more intensive working and delayed maintenance. Moreover, in the immediate aftermath of the war railway finances deteriorated markedly: the threat of major bankruptcies effectively ruled out a simple return to the pre-war situation.[51] Furthermore, the war had demonstrated the advantages of unified and co-operative working of the railways. The Select Committee on Transport in 1918 had already indicated that 'unification of the railway system is desirable under suitable safeguards, whether the ownership be in public or private hands.'[52] The key question was, therefore, by what means could the benefits of unified operation best be retained in the aftermath of war-time government control?

Public ownership of the railways was an emotive and politically sensitive issue. It had been raised as a serious possibility on only one previous occasion when, in 1844, a House of Commons Select Committee had recommended that the state should have powers to purchase the railways after fifteen years.[53] Subsequent opposition from the group of railway directors in Parliament – the railway interest as it was called – ensured that the public ownership clauses of the subsequent Railway Act of 1844 were much diluted and unlikely to be invoked.[54] It was not until the era of reconstruction after the war that government began to seriously reconsider the case for public ownership.

The Labour Party and trade unions were already committed to nationalisation. At cabinet level both the Prime Minister, Lloyd George, and Winston Churchill had made recent statements which could be interpreted as offering support for public ownership. Even the railway companies themselves, though hostile to nationalisation, thought a return to the pre-war situation unrealistic. But by 1920 the chances of the Coalition Government adopting public ownership as the solution to the railway's problems were fading. With the social and industrial unrest of 1919–20 receding the Government's thinking became clearer. Under the influence of Sir Eric Geddes, the first Minister of Transport, the amalgamation of the railways into seven large groups (later reduced to four) was envisaged.[55]

The intention of grouping was primarily to preserve private control of the railways. Through large-scale amalgamation the government hoped to secure several improvements in railway operation and finances which would ensure a return to profitability and long term stability. Through a greater degree of unified operation 'wasteful competition' would be eliminated, while it was expected that further economies would result from the standardisation of equipment and co-operative working. In addition to reorganisation it was intended that the Minister of Transport would be given new regulatory powers, particularly in the important areas of railway facilities and charging. This would secure the public interest at the same time as allowing the companies to gear their operations and charges to the achievement of an annual net revenue comparable to that of 1913.[56]

These proposals were ultimately embodied in the Railways Act of 1921. For the railway companies compulsory amalgamation was more palatable than nationalisation and could be interpreted as a partial victory for private enterprise. Public control of the railways would be increased, yet Parliament had now sanctioned on a massive scale the amalgamation process eagerly followed by the companies before the war. For the supporters of nationalisation, however, the Act represented a huge opportunity lost. Expressing the dissatisfaction of many on his own side of the House, the Labour Member J. R. Clynes dismissed the Bill as 'a piece of makeshift . . . a rank and uncompromising experiment [which would] only increase the clash between public interest and private greed.'[57]

Certainly the Act did not eliminate competition between the railway companies. Although the groups were in theory territorial monopolies, in practice competition was preserved to a remarkable degree, particularly on services between London and the larger cities and on a range of cross-country services.[58] Of course, in some cases competition for traffic produced lower fares for passengers. But it was all rather haphazard and uncoordinated. Indeed, it was significant that the machinery for dealing with rates and charges created under the legislation of 1921 was of little relevance to the question of passenger fares, the companes being left with considerable freedom to determine their charges.[59]

But perhaps the most serious deficiency of the grouping was that it proved irrelevant to the growing need for greater coordination of transport services. Although it was still possible for the railways to exploit their regional monopoly on some routes, in practice the growth of competing road (and air) transport services contributed a new dimension to the problem of competition which the Act had not foreseen. The only effective answer to wasteful competition was a greater degree of coordination and public control of transport. During the 1930s there were portents of a more comprehensive approach to the problem in the London Passenger Transport Act of 1933 and legislation in other transport sectors. However, it was to take the impact of the Second World War and a second extended period of government control of transport to advance the cause of unification and public ownership.

By the end of the war the credibility of a return to private ownership of the railways had been destroyed. The Transport Act of 1947, passed by Attlee's Labour government, transferred to public ownership and control the railways along with other major sectors of inland transport. In place of a dependence upon market forces and competition, nationalisation opened up the prospect of a comprehensive and coordinated approach to the provision of transport services. If the legislation was vague on how these laudable objectives were to be achieved it nevertheless marked the start of a new era in the relationship between government, the railway and its passengers.

Our concern in this chapter has been to highlight those aspects of railway construction and operation which demanded intervention by the state on behalf of the general public interest and the specific interests of the railway passenger. Perhaps the most fundamental of these related to the desirability of entrusting railways to private enterprise. Until public ownership in 1947 the services the passenger received, their cost and the safety with which they were attended were determined ultimately by the railway companies themselves. Yet unbridled free enterprise was rejected by the state and these key aspects of railway travel were influenced to varying degrees by state interference. However, regulation of the railways evolved in an *ad hoc*, piecemeal fashion, the state largely reacting to events or interfering only when the case had become so overwhelming that it could no longer be ignored.

Parliamentary consideration of railway problems was subject to a variety of often conflicting pressures. The electoral fortunes of the major parties; the power of the railway interest in parliament; the attitudes of Board of Trade officials; the influence of public opinion; the burden of government business; the incidence of war: all these factors were to play a part in shaping the ultimate form and timing of government regulation. The result was always likely to be a compromise which for some represented too much interference, for others too little and too late. This was the fundamental problem facing government in its attempts to formulate consistent policies on railway matters. It was difficult to satisfy simultaneously the interests of the industry, its passengers or the state because, as the railway analyst William Galt observed, those interests were frequently opposed.

3
Connecting the Towns:
The Development of Main Line
Passenger Services

> When Pickwick began to appear in 1836, though the air was full of
> railway projects, England of the roads was almost untouched. Gig
> and coach, oastler and guard, and the great ritual of changing horses,
> seemed barely threatened. . . . But the projectors and constructors
> were at work, and their leaders already had in mind not just railways
> but a railway system.
>
> J. H. Clapham

The years between 1830 and the 1850s formed a seminal period in
the development of Britain's railways. Firstly, during these years the
outline of the railway map was clearly established. Subsequent
additions to the total railway mileage were considerable, but the
basic pattern of trunk routes established by the 1850s remained
unaltered. Secondly, and closely related, was the construction of the
major Victorian railway stations. Vital as they were to the start and
finish of railway journeys, the siting of the major city termini, like
the building of the main lines themselves, was determined by a
complex of factors, only one of which was the convenience of
prospective passengers. Thirdly, these years saw the main line
companies expand their empires and gain experience of the long-
distance passenger business. Forthly, it was during these formative
years of operation that class-based passenger services were
established as one of the most enduring features of British railway
travel. In more ways than one, therefore, the constructional phase
of railway activity was to have a lasting influence on both the
railway and its passengers. Before tracing the development of main
line passenger services, we need to explore in greater detail the
legacy of these years.

"THE CORONATION"

THE FIRST STREAMLINE TRAIN
KING'S CROSS FOR SCOTLAND

WEEKDAYS (Except Saturdays and Public Holidays)

King's Cross	- -	dep.	4. 0 p.m.
York	- - -	,,	6. 40 p.m.
Edinburgh (Waverley)	- - -	arr.	10. 0 p.m.
Edinburgh (Waverley)	- - -	dep.	4. 30 p.m.
Newcastle	- - -	,,	6. 33 p.m.
King's Cross	- -	arr.	10. 30 p.m.

IT'S QUICKER BY RAIL

LONDON & NORTH EASTERN RAILWAY

One of the premier main line railway services heavily advertised by the LNER in the later 1930s (by permission of the BRB).

46

The Main Line System and the Passenger

By 1871, with over 15,000 route miles open for traffic, the railway map showed 'not just the outline, but the detail of the twentieth century system.'[1] Although railway construction was not yet at an end, the essential framework of trunk lines connecting the cities and most of the major towns had been completed. The detailed chronology of development is not important in this context, but the general pattern of growth may be summarised in the following terms: 'The first trunk routes were from the north-west to the midlands; and from the midlands to London; then followed the north-east to the midlands to London, then the midlands to Bristol, London to Bristol. [2]

The shape and size of the railway network owed little to rational planning or any agreed scale of social and economic priorities. As we have seen parliament was unwilling, often incapable, of pursuing a coherent policy and much was left to the forces of enterprise, haste and greed. In theory the promoters of railway schemes had to demonstrate to parliament that their line would fulfil a genuine need for both passenger and goods transport. In practice their depositions were often framed in the most general terms. Estimating capital costs was relatively straightforward, but forecasting the traffic and profitability of a projected line was altogether more difficult. Professional traffic-takers could be employed to assess existing traffic along particular routeways, but a scrutiny of the public accounts of canal companies or a simple count of vehicles provided little reliable guide to the number of *new* passengers who might be attracted to a railway.[3]

For these reasons the earliest promoters were tentative about the prospects for generating passenger traffic, relying more on faith than fact. 'Select your termini', observed the early railway historian F. S. Williams, 'and run your lines between them as straight as you can. It is not even necessary that there should be a single home upon the route. Open the line, and as people flock to the banks of that first great highway, a river, so they will flock (we are assured) to your railway.'[4] The parody was not without foundation: although the difficulties of making accurate forecasts of passenger traffic remained, already by the late 1830s parliamentary committees were taking it for granted that the opening of a new line would double at least the number of people previously travelling by road.[5] As the large main line companies began to dominate the industry, the pattern of railway development became increasingly dependent upon the outcome of a series of power struggles which afflicted both boardrooms and parliamentary committees.

These contests for control of the great trunk routes, likened by one authoritative study of transport history to a 'species of imperialism', went beyond considerations of earning a reasonable return on capital.[6] The determination to exclude a rival company from one's own 'territory' or the ability to appease landowners and others who might begin from a stance of opposition to a particular railway scheme often dominated the process of route selection. Certainly the opposition of landowners could be time consuming and costly. To prevent such opposition reaching parliament railway companies were sometimes prepared to pay landowners considerable sums in 'compensation'. The Lancaster & Carlisle Railway, for example, bought off one potential opponent with £3,000 for a mere acre of ground. But occasionally even this device failed to dislodge the entrenched opponent. The classic case was Lord FitzWilliam, an inveterate enemy of the proposed Great Northern Railway from London to York, who claimed his object was 'merely to prevent the separation of some woods which in a hunting point of view are inseparable.'[7]

Nevertheless, the extent of oppositon of this kind should not be exaggerated. Frequently landowners objected not because they opposed all railways, but because they felt that their district would be inadequately served by a proposed railway or, worse still, not served at all. The trading community was often at the forefront of such opposition; in the case of Northampton, for instance, complaining that the projected route of the London & Birmingham intended by-passing the town. Although landowners could and did influence the choice of route, their opposition to any railway scheme was tempered by an awareness of local opinion. As one historian of landed society has observed: 'It is apparent that anxiety to protect residential pleasures had to be balanced against the desire not to inflame local feelings, and the notion of the landowners' complete opposition to the early railways must be qualified accordingly.'[8] Opposition was in any case never confined to landowners, those with vested interests – canal companies, coach proprietors, waggoners, innkeepers and even other railway companies – usually provided the stiffest opposition to projected railway schemes.

However, in the urban environment, the pattern of landownership often played a crucial role in railway development and route selection. As the major companies jostled with each other to forge independent lines through the urban fringes towards more favoured 'central' station sites the stakes for companies and landowners alike grew higher. No self-respecting company with designs on lucrative main line passenger traffic could afford to be without its own access into the hearts of the cities. Agreements to share the tracks of another company, though often resorted to, were no substitute for possession of an independent route and, at the end of it, a station worthy of the company's name.

The companies were prepared to lavish a great deal of attention and money on their city terminals. They wanted imposing structures to reflect the status and prestige of the company – to instil in those who saw and used them feelings of 'admiration, respect, and confidence'.[9] The land hunger of the major companies and the capital costs of urban railway projects were enormous. Moreover, as traffic grew, it was often essential for further extensions to track, station and ancillary facilities all of which required more land, often at premium prices: for example, over £1 million for the LSWR's extension from Nine Elms to Waterloo and £4 million for the SER's Charing Cross and Cannon Street.[10]

All this could be to the advantage of urban landowners, although it was usually the largest who had most to gain. On the basis of a study of railway development in the major cities, Dr Kellett has shown that the companies preferred dealing with a few large estate owners rather than a multiplicity of small owners. This speeded up negotiations, reduced the chances of litigation and, above all, proved cheaper than a string of separate settlements. But the large estate owner's gain was invariably the poor tenant's loss: railways tended to blaze their way through the residential districts of the working class, across land that was usually relatively low in value and held in large blocks by a single owner. Estimates of the number of Londoners alone dispossessed by railway construction during the nineteenth century vary from 76,000 to 120,000.[11]

Yet the results of all this expenditure and endeavour were, from the point of view of both companies and passengers, often disappointing. The Great Northern's experience with its London terminus at King's Cross was one of the most unfortunate. Opened in 1852 the station was cramped and the approach lines, through the Gas Works and Copenhagen tunnels, steeply graded. Passenger train arrivals and departures, light engines and empty coach movements often conflicted with each other and with traffic to the nearby freight terminals. As traffic grew from the original 26 trains a day to 309 by 1909 the station was extended and the layout revised on three separate occasions. However, King's Cross station and its approaches, especially the 'neck of a bottle' at Finsbury Park, remained awkward and expensive to operate.[12]

Like King's Cross, many of the earlier city terminals were built out of the centre on what was then the edge of the urban area. Subsequently the railways made determined attempts to secure more central and prestigious sites for terminal stations. In London, where the City authorities were in any case hostile to intrusions by railways, this set the scene for a series of protracted struggles as the companies tried to encroach into the City itself. The SER, for instance, lobbied hard for permission to extend to London Bridge and Charing Cross during the 1850s, its supporters claiming it would be of:

> much convenience to the highest classes of society – the nobility, gentry, members of Parliament and their families . . . enabling them to arrive in town in the season, and to leave it when it is over for their residences, or for sea-bathing quarters, or for the continent, without passing through the crowded thoroughfares of the East End.[13]

Having carefully oriented its campaign towards those involved in the decision making process the SER duly obtained powers to build its extension in 1859. Other companies followed: by the end of the century London had six terminals within the area of the City, although none, with the exception of Charing Cross, could be described as truly central. The major provincial cities and towns often shared, on a smaller scale, the problem of the proliferation and peripheral location of terminal stations. By the time of the Grouping, for instance, the city of Manchester had five main line stations. There were exceptions – Newcastle, York, Carlisle, Aberdeen and several others had their passenger services concentrated in one major station. But in the main, the forces of competition and independence ensured the construction of several separate stations. The inconvience to passengers is readily apparent since few did not require some additional transport to begin, end or simply continue their journey.

As the cities expanded beyond the limits of the old 'walking city' this was perhaps inevitable. But the paradox of the railway was that while it made journeys over long distances infinitely quicker, in the city it contributed to the confusion and congestion of the streets and frequently made movement much more difficult. The vast numbers arriving, departing and waiting at stations placed enormous strains on intra-urban transport. The stations were the focal points for an array of passenger services – hansoms, hackneys, omnibuses and later trams – and were also the destination for an even greater range of carting services in connection with mail, parcels, luggage and goods. Small wonder that the number of horses employed in road haulage more than doubled to well over 3 million during the course of Victoria's reign.[14]

In addition hotels, small retail outlets and catering establishments were soon attracted to sites close to the stations where a large transient population was guaranteed. The railway companies contributed to this process by providing their own hotel accommodation. Station hotels at Euston and Curzon Street (Birmingham) built in the 1830s were among the earliest but were soon followed by other, increasingly palatial, railway owned hotels at many of the major city terminals.[15] The crowded thoroughfares leading to the stations and their hotels was testimony to the railway's importance as a generator of street traffic, both pedestrian and vehicular.

Yet the railway held out one possible solution to the problem it had helped to create. In London, where traffic congestion was acute, the opening of the Metropolitan Railway in 1863 established the feasibility of carrying the railway into the heart of the city yet conveniently hidden underground. As the network of underground lines developed cross-city travel was undoubtedly made easier – although the long-distance passenger with heavy luggage may not have agreed. But as an approach to the traffic problem it was not the answer. Few of London's underground lines confined themselves to the role of moving people around the inner city. They rapidly

THE ROYAL SCOT

14th June to 19th September inclusive 1954

WEEKDAYS

NORTHBOUND

LONDON (Euston) ... dep. 10 00 am
GLASGOW (Central) arr.   5†15 pm

SOUTHBOUND

GLASGOW (Central) dep. 10 00 am
LONDON (Euston) ... arr.   5†15 pm

　　　　　†6 00 pm on Saturdays.

SUNDAYS

NORTHBOUND

LONDON (Euston) ... dep. 10 00 am
GLASGOW (Central) arr.   7 45 pm

SOUTHBOUND

GLASGOW (Central) dep. 11 15 am
LONDON (Euston) ... arr.   8 00 pm

The journey from Euston to Glasgow Central includes stops at certain stations. For details see time-tables.

RESERVATION OF SEATS

Seats can be reserved in advance, fee 1/- per seat, at the seat reservation offices at Euston and other London terminal stations, Glasgow (Central) station, or through the usual travel agencies.

FARES

The fares between London (Euston) and Glasgow (Central) are as under :—

	1st class		3rd class	
	Single	Return	Single	Return
	88/-	176/-	58/8	117/4

Children 3 years and under 14 years of age half fare.

The above fares are liable to alteration.

MEALS

Luncheon and Afternoon Tea on the journey can be obtained in the refreshment car. Light refreshments and a corridor service are made available whenever practicable.

The Royal Scot normally leaves Euston from platform 13 and Glasgow (Central) from platform 2.

By the 1950s the railways had still not recovered from the ravages of the Second World War. As this 1954 advertisement for services on the West Coast main line suggests, speeds and journey times were still considerably inferior to those offered to the pre-War passenger.

pushed out feeder lines into the suburbs and, like their main line bretheren, made a major contribution to street traffic, particularly in the vicinity of the stations. The underground option was in any case confined to London, although later Liverpool with the Mersey Railway, and Glasgow with the Cathcart Circle line, developed minor variants.

The Development of Main Line Passenger Services

At this point it is worth elucidating a question which has already been approached indirectly in previous pages. What sort of services did the railway companies offer to the passenger and how did they respond to changes in the pattern of demand for travel? When the first long distance trunk lines – the Grand Junction and London & Birmingham – began operations passenger services were fairly restricted. The Grand Junction, opened in 1837, provided passengers with a choice of either first class or mixed trains for the 82½ miles journey between Curzon Street and Newton on the Liverpool & Manchester line. First class trains consisted of 'coaches carrying six inside, and of Mails carrying four inside, one compartment of which is convertible into a Bed-carriage, if required.' Mixed trains comprised both first- and second-class coaches, 'the latter affording complete protection from the weather, and differing only from the First Class in having no lining, cushions, or divisions of the compartments.' Initially the company made no provision for third-class passengers. Fares for the through journey between Birmingham and Liverpool/Manchester were 40s for a bed-carriage, 25s for a mail coach seat, 21s for a first-class seat and 14s in second class.[16]

The London & Birmingham Railway, opened shortly after the Grand Junction, offered three classes of accommodation from the start, an advantage partially offset by a complicated fares structure. This distinguished between day and night travel and the density of carriage seating. Third-class passengers were charged a single fare of 14s for a seat in an uncovered vehicle – the same as the second-class fare charged by the Grand Junction. The Great Western's important line between London and Bristol, opened in 1841, also made provision for third-class travel, but the emphasis was overwhelmingly on first and second. By 1846 the Select Committee on Railway Acts Enactments could observe of the neglect of third-class facilities by most of the major companies that 'it appeared as if it had been determined to exclude the great body of the nation, unable of course to pay first and second class fares, from the benefit communicated to the more wealthy orders.'[17]

Another feature of railway services by the 1840s was their restricted number – a much less intensive service being available on most lines than the dozen or so trains run by the L&MR during the early 1830s. From Euston the L&BR despatched thirteen trains daily to Birmingham and received fourteen in return. The GJR ran six trains daily in each direction, as did the North Midland Railway between Derby and Leeds. The GWR's Paddington terminus handled a similar number of trains as Euston, but only six trains a day ran the whole distance to Bristol. South of the Thames, both the LSWR's line from Nine Elms to Southampton and the LBSC's line to Brighton carried seven trains each way. In Scotland, the most important route between Glasgow and Edinburgh offered six return journeys. On all these lines Sunday services were much curtailed. The L&BR, which offered rather more Sunday trains than most, ran only five in each direction.[18]

From the 1850s, with demand for travel facilities increasing rapidly, there was a steady rise in the number of main line trains. The most significant improvements, as the Royal Commission on Railways in 1867 recognised, took place on routes with competing lines, such as London to Scotland, Manchester, Liverpool and Leeds. For instance, by the 1880s passengers between Liverpool and London could choose from 28 trains daily, 13 on the LNWR, 9 on the Midland and 6 on the GNR. From London to Manchester 32 trains were available, 16 on the LNWR and 8 each on the Midland and GNR. In addition these companies, in conjunction with their Scottish allies, were running around 20 trains a day from London to Scotland.[19] Nonetheless, long-distance trains of the express or semi-fast variety comprised only a portion of the increase in total main line traffic. Much was local traffic, especially to the suburbs, or excursion traffic. Such trains made use of main line tracks and stations for all or part of their journeys. Indeed, one of the principal features of railway travel in mid-Victorian years was the growing importance of short-distance traffic. In the 1840s the average length of journey was 15–16 miles. By 1870 it had fallen to 10 miles.[20]

Short distance and third class: these were the principal features of the growth in total railway passenger traffic during the second half of the nineteenth century. But for all this, it was the prestige end of the market – first-class passengers conveyed by faster, long-distance trains – which arguably dominated the operations of the leading companies. As the *Quarterly Review* sardonically remarked:

> Everything must give way to them. Coal and goods trains are shunted – parliamentary trains are drawn into sidings – and signals are manned to clear the road and signal it 'all clear' for the 'down' or 'up' express. Chairmen are almost ready to weep when they hear of an accident befalling them. Yet it is doubtful whether, in many cases, the express defrays the cost of working it.[21]

Speed was certainly soon recognised as an important component of passenger custom. The GWR, with its Exeter expresses, was the first to run a daily, non-stop train over distances of fifty miles or more. They began running in 1845, timetabled to run the 194 miles from Paddington to Exeter in 5 hours – an average of 43 mph. The introduction of this service was largely a response to criticisms of the slow speed of GWR expresses and provided an opportunity for the company to show what the broad gauge could do in view of the impending 'battle of the gauges' in parliament. But it was no flash in the pan: by late 1847 the fastest expresses were covering the distance in 4hr 25min.[22]

Meanwhile, on the 'narrow' gauge, speeds were also being increased. The LSWR introduced an express service between London and Southampton in 1845. The following year the London & Birmingham also began running fast expresses. Out of Euston these required the assistance of a pilot engine attached to the front of the train. Having completed its task the pilot was detached at speed by the fireman who was obliged to clamber onto the back of the tender. The pilot engine was then accelerated ahead of the express and diverted into a siding, the points being immediately re-set to allow the train to thunder through on the main line. Incredibly, it seems that this hazardous operation was regularly performed without any serious mishap.

From the 1850s the force of competition produced further improvements in express train services. The recently formed LNWR, for example, waged a battle with its competitors on the

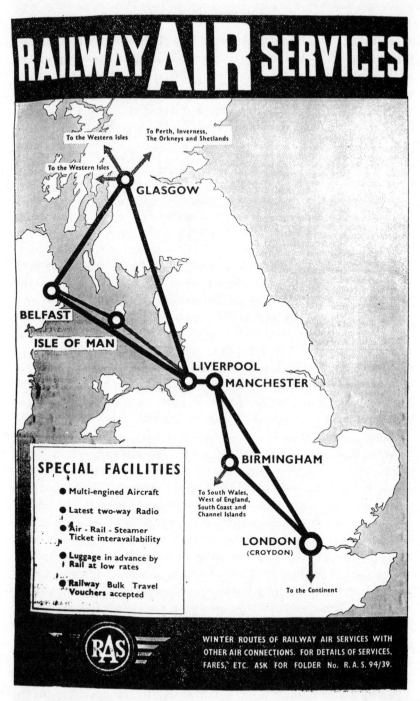

One of the major responses of the railways to the growth of competition from internal air services between the Wars was to enter the field themselves. The GWR inaugurated the first railway air services in 1933 and in the following year Railway Air Services Ltd was established to provide all four railway companies with services on certain major routes.

routes to the Midlands, Lancashire and Scotland. Their expresses were originally intended as prestige trains offering tactical advantages over the GWR and GNR services, but from the mid-1850s the company was also extending their appeal by including second-class carriages. On the competing West and East Coast routes to Scotland the battle was also hotting up. With best journey times between London and Edinburgh on the East Coast route down from 12½ hours to 11 hours by 1852–3 the West Coast companies responded with a similar cut. Thereafter the battle shifted towards extending accommodation for second- and third-class passengers.[23]

However, during the later 1850s and 1860s competition became rather less aggressive as the general managers who belonged to the Railway Clearing House scheme began to shift the emphasis towards greater co-operation. Thus, in the spring of 1867 they agreed to reduce speeds and increase journey times by specified amounts on a route by route basis. From London to Birmingham 10min were added; London to Sheffield 12min; London to Manchester, Leeds, Bradford and York, 15min; London to Edinburgh and Glasgow 30min. The speed of other fast trains was also to be reduced 'where any question of competition was involved', the various traffic superintendents being given the task of bringing the new arrangements into effect.[24]

Collusion between the companies to preserve the traditional exclusivity of travel on long-distance expresses is also evident around this time. It was agreed to limit facilities for third-class passengers on trains travelling in excess of 75 miles with a recommendation that there should be not more than two third-class trains daily in each direction. To prevent further dilution of passenger class distinctions it was agreed that the practice of allowing third-class passengers to actually ride in second-class carriages also be abandoned.[25]

Although the third-class passenger seems to have suffered by these agreements, in the longer term a measure of co-operation between the companies was essential for the satisfactory working of long-distance trains. In the early years the relatively small average route mileage of each company (still only 41 miles by 1846) and the fierce independence of the companies made both through booking and the running of through trains difficult. 'I came up to London in the middle of January', complained one traveller from Preston in 1839, 'and was very desirous . . . to come through in one carriage. . . . I found there was no chance of it, and that I could only book to Parkside, then from Parkside I had to book again to Birmingham, and the inconvenience was so great at Birmingham that I had no time to get refreshment properly, having to look after my luggage.'[26] The guilty parties in this instance – the North Union, GJR and L&MR – were soon to arrive at an agreement to obviate such difficulties and allow passengers 'without changing their carriage or their seat [to be] comfortably transported from Preston to London or *vice versa*.'[27]

The establishment in 1842 of the railway Clearing House was intended to increase the opportunities for arrangements of this kind. Member companies soon began work establishing rules for the handling of through passenger traffic, a major breakthrough being a scheme under which collected tickets returned to the Clearing House by the companies entitled them to a portion of the receipts according to distances travelled on each railway. Better ticketing systems, notably Edmondson's, which reduced opportunities for fraud and evasion facilitated the extension of this scheme. Greater efforts to co-ordinate timetables from the 1850s also did much to ease long journeys involving changes of trains, while the running of through carriages was facilitated by an agreement to charge a penny per mile for each borrowed coach while it was on 'foreign' lines.[28]

Although a great deal still remained to be done, the Clearing House undoubtedly made through booking easier. Rivalry between the companies remained a considerable obstacle and cases are legend of passengers being sent by zealous booking clerks on circuitous journeys which avoided more direct routes owned by competitors. Cross-country journeys remained the most problematical, the passenger having to wait until relatively late in the century for an expansion in these services. The Great Central Railway – latecomer among the main line companies – fulfilled an important role in this respect because of its connections with most of the leading companies. Early in the twentieth century the GCR introduced some notable cross-country services, such as those linking Newcastle with Cardiff and Bournemouth. However, the extent of long-distance passenger travel – cross-country or otherwise – should not be exaggerated. Receipts from 'through' traffic between companies formed only some 14 per cent of total passenger receipts for most of the nineteenth century while, as we have seen, the average length of journey fell during the course of the century.[29]

Improvements in Carriage Design and Passenger Amenities

Early railway carriages were based on their road transport predecessors. The superstructure was essentially a stretched road mail coach divided into two or three compartments. Outside the typical carriage had a boot at one end, luggage racks on the roof and an elevated position for the guard. The wooden body sat on iron frames and ran on four wheels. Inside the first-class passenger was provided with upholstered bench seats arranged transversely; second class was much less comfortable – wooden seats and open sides, but at least roofed. Third-class accommodation took the form of open trucks, occasionally without seats, but usually with backless benches.

Over the years carriage standards improved only gradually, the carriages of mid-century being little removed from the early vehicles. Arguably the most significant changes occurred in third class following Gladstone's Act of 1844 which at least gave this class of passenger protection from the weather. However, by the 1850s passengers of all classes could count themselves unlucky to find a carriage without sprung wheels and buffers. In addition, first- and second-class compartments were usually provided with an oil lamp, third-class usually one per carriage. Heating was even more discriminatory. The Great Northern pioneered the use of 'footwarmers' – metal containers periodically replenished with boiling water (later soda crystals were used requiring the containers to be periodically shaken to reactive the heat-giving solution). Inefficient and labour intensive, footwarmers were adopted by all the leading companies, although they were initially reserved for those first-class passengers prepared to pay a supplementary charge.[30]

The most striking advances in carriage design and passenger amenities came during the last quarter of the nineteenth century. The pace setter was the Midland Railway. In 1872 the company decided to carry third-class passengers on all its trains and the following year began improving the standard of third-class carriages notably by providing upholstered seats. Then, in 1875, the Midland abolished all second-class accommodation on its trains, at the same time reducing first-class fares. Meanwhile, the company began to switch from rigid wheelbase vehicles to bogie coaches with the introduction of Pullman services on several routes during the mid-1870s. The American style Pullman had better riding qualities than traditional designs and offered passengers a range of amenities such as dining facilities, lavatories, through corridors, kerosene lighting and hot water heating.[31]

The Midland's decision to abolish second class was gradually followed by its competitors. Edward Watkin's pithy observation that the Pullmans represented the Midland's first class, the first class the equivalent of class two and third of class three was not shared by the rest of the industry.[32] By the time of the Grouping second class had all but disappeared from the railway system, although it could still be found in isolated areas such as the South Eastern & Chatham lines. Following the Midland's lead, comfort and amenities also began to supplant price as the major tools in the competitive battle for passengers. As the manager of the LNWR recognised: 'it requires but a trifling inducement to influence the travelling public in the choice of route, so that there is a constant temptation to the competing companies to make fresh concessions so as to attract the business from their rivals.'[33] Dining and refreshment cars, sleeping cars, corridors between and within carriages, steam heating, gas and later electric lighting were introduced by most of the main line companies during the later nineteenth and early twentieth centuries.

The initiative did not always come from the Midland. In the case of restaurant car services on ordinary trains the GNR led, introducing them on its London–Leeds trains in 1879. The concept of a table d'hote meal on the move was far removed from the compulsory refreshment stops of earlier years at places such as Preston, York, Normanton and the much dreaded Swindon Junction Hotel. Popular with the travelling public, the range of restaurant car services expanded rapidly. By 1913 a total of 457 restaurant car expresses were run each day, the LNWR alone serving some one million meals a year on its trains.[34]

During the early years of the twentieth century carriage designs changed considerably, setting standards which were to last for thirty years or more. In 1905 both the GWR and GNR broke with recent practice, replacing the high clerestory with the elliptical roof. Churchward's Dreadnought carriages for the GWR were built on a grand scale – the largest yet to run in ordinary service – and were notable for replacing individual doors to the compartments with access from an internal side corridor. Gresley's designs for the GNR were equally innovative – steel underframes, teak bodies, wide corridor connections and automatic couplers. New they may have been, but the carriages of these years retained the air of handcrafted products: wooden bodies, sweeping curves, intricate panelling and handwork, lavish painting and lining and protected by numerous coats of varnish. Only the roughness of ride on some lines, caused by imperfections in the track, served to remind of earlier and more rudimentary days of railway travel.

One of the most significant features of the development of long-distance services during the late Victorian period was the improvement in third class standards. By the late 1880s most express trains included third-class carriages in their formation.[35] After the Midland's pioneering contribution interior comfort improved markedly. Upholstered seats, dining and refreshment facilities and lavatories were increasingly made available to the third-class passenger. Such improvements were partly the result of competitive pressures, but they were also a reflection of the changing nature of the passenger market. With a falling cost of living and rising real wages for those in work during the last quarter of the nineteenth century, travel became increasingly accessible to a wider cross-section of the population. It was no coincidence, for example, that the 1880s and 1890s saw the extensive development of the working-class holiday market, a market which was heavily dependent upon travel by train. Like several other business enterprises of the period, the railways were beginning to discover the true potential of a mass domestic market.[36] Fuelled by the abolition of second-class accommodation the importance of third-class traffic grew. Between 1874 and 1888 the mean percentage of passengers travelling third class on four of the leading companies increased from 80 to 91 per cent, while the equivalent figure for first class fell from 20 to 9 per cent.[37]

The changing structure of railway passenger traffic reveals the initiatives of the Midland Railway for what they were: a bold but essentially rational assessment of the growing importance of third-class travel. James Allport, the company's astute chairman, was never anxious to refute suggestions that his decision owed something to altruism – an attempt to confer on the poor of the land 'a mighty boon' as F. S. Williams expressed it. Yet the rationale behind the Midland's business strategy was strictly commercial with more than a hint of political economy thrown in for good measure. 'When a poor man travels', Allport observed, 'he has not only to pay his fare but to sink his capital, for his time is his capital; and if he now consumes only five hours instead of ten in making his journey, he has saved five hours of time for useful labour – useful to himself, to his family, and to society.'[38]

Paradoxically there were also commercial reasons why some of the Midland's competitors were not always prepared to embrace a new age of high volume, lower margin business with open arms. With total passenger traffic increasing considerably – a four-fold increase between 1870 and 1914 – existing track capacity and facilities on the main lines were often no longer adequate. Extra traffic required extensions to track and stations, longer and more frequent trains, faster and more powerful engines. Each required a considerable outlay of capital and higher day-to-day running costs. Nor should we under-estimate class snobbery among railway leaders as a source of opposition to extending third-class facilities. Watkin, never afraid to express an opinion, declared as 'a great public injustice' the Midland's policy of 'driving together classes who do not naturally wish to associate.'[39]

Under different circumstances the companies might have preferred to retain the traditional lower volume, higher margin business. By the late-Victorian period this was no longer feasible. As one historian has argued, the railways 'were in too vulnerable a position competitively and politically for them to risk turning away additional traffic or even to neglect the improvement of services in order to attract it.'[40] In a sense the railways were victims of the increased demand for travelling, forced to accept by parliament and public something akin to a 'public service' role under which they behaved more like public corporations than profit making organisations.[41]

FURNESS RAILWAY

1st and 3rd Class
Cheap Day Tickets
(By Specified Ordinary Trains).

EVERY DAY
(Bank & other Holidays excepted),

FROM AND TO

Ambleside	Haverthwaite
Arnside	Heversham
Bootle	Kents Bank
Bowness	Kirkby
Broughton	Lakeside
Cark	Ravenglass
Drigg	St. Bees
Coniston	Seascale
Furness Abbey	Silecroft
Grange	Silverdale
Greenodd	Torver

AND

The Furness Coast, The Lake Stations and Furness Abbey,

All the Year Round.

EVERY DAY (Including Sundays.)

MAY, JUNE, JULY, AUGUST & SEPTEMBER
(Bank and other Holidays excepted).

1st and 3rd Class
Cheap Day Tickets
(MINIMUM FARE 6d.)

By Specified Ordinary Trains,
ARE ISSUED

FROM	TO
Barrow	Coniston
Roose	Lake Side
Askam	Bowness
Millom	Ambleside, &c.
Dalton	The Furness
Lindal	Coast Stations
Ulverston	AND
Whitehaven	Furness Abbey

* Not issued to Furness Abbey from these Stations.

From OCTOBER 1st to APRIL 30th
THESE TICKETS WILL BE ISSUED EVERY
Monday, Saturday & † Sunday, and on the Tradesmen's Weekly Holiday,
* Not to Bowness and Ambleside on Sundays, October 1st to May 31st.

CHEAP
WEEK-END TICKETS

Available on any Ordinary Train having a through connection every

Friday, Saturday and Sunday,
ALL THE YEAR ROUND,

AVAILABLE TO RETURN ON

SUNDAY, and the following
MONDAY and TUESDAY

FROM THE

PRINCIPAL TOWNS

TO THE

PLEASURE RESORTS,

FROM ALL THE

the Furness Railway.

CHEAP
WEEKLY TICKETS
(1st AND 3rd CLASS),
ARE ISSUED BETWEEN

ANY TWO STATIONS
ON THE
FURNESS RAILWAY,
AVAILABLE FOR

SIX RETURN JOURNEYS
By any Ordinary Train at a charge of
Six Ordinary Single Fares
With certain exceptions for the Week.

Minimum Charge :—1st Class, 4 -. 3rd Class, 2 -: Children under 12 years of age, Half-price.

These Tickets will all terminate within seven days of the date of issue, and no allowance will be made for journeys not travelled. The use of a Ticket to or from an intermediate Station will constitute the journey.

The Six Return Journeys can be made at any time during the week.
The Tickets are not Transferable, and the name of the passenger entitled to the use of the Ticket will be written thereon. Applications for Tickets to be made at the Booking Offices.

Alfred Aslett, Secretary
and General Manager.

As this collection of 'cheap' travel facilities offered by the Furness Railway suggests an increasingly complex fares structure was becoming the norm on many railways even before the Grouping of 1923.

In this way the third-class passenger benefitted, but the gap between the two main classes of travel remained considerable. Belying the relative importance of third- and first-class passenger receipts to their fortunes, the railways of the pre-First World War period continued to shower the latest innovations and comforts on the first-class traveller long before they filtered down to third class. This contradition in railway policy was neatly summed up by the general manager of the LNWR:

> the companies have spent and are spending large sums of money in providing the most luxurious accommodation and every facility and convenience for the benefit of the superior classes, but they are doing this practically at their own expense, and it is the humble and once despised third class traveller who furnishes the sinews of war.[42]

Train Services in the Twentieth Century

By the Edwardian age main line trains had become longer and heavier, carrying many more passengers in greater comfort and safety. In addition, the fastest expresses were travelling at higher speeds. Since the 1870s speed had been subject to the same competitive pressures as other passenger facilities. Foxwell and Farrar, who meticulously studied train speeds in the later Victorian period, showed that between 1871 and 1888 both the total number of express services and the total daily mileage of such trains increased between two and three fold. By the early years of the new century the timetables offered a remarkable collection of express train services each running non-stop over distances of 100 miles or more. In 1907 there were 157 such trains; by 1913 there were 193.[43]

The LNWR provided the most comprehensive service of expresses with 64 daily runs over 100 miles or more. This was followed by the GWR with 43 runs, the GNR with 29, the Midland with 20, the NER with 13, the Caledonian with 8, the GER with 7, the GCR with 5 and the LSWR with 4. The use of slip coaches attached to the rear of the train allowed intermediate stations to be served without the express itself stopping. Before the First World War the highest speed was achieved by the GWR with a start to stop average of 59.4mph on its London to Bath expresses (by slip carriage). The best speeds of the remaining companies were not far short of this: only the GER (49.9mph London–Trowse) and the

Caledonian (49.5mph Carlisle–Perth) falling below a 50mph average. By 1914 the fastest services from London to the major cities showed some remarkable improvements over the early days of the railways: from London to Birmingham the fastest journey took just 2hr, a reduction of 1hr 55min on the best time in 1844; to Liverpool it was 3hr 35min, a reduction of 4hr 40min; to Bristol it was 2hr, a reduction of 2hr 20min; and to Leeds 3hr 25min, a reduction of 5hr 20min.[44]

The First World War put a stop to these exploits. With many expresses converted to stopping services or simply withdrawn, travelling times increased considerably during the war. Trains were often severely overcrowded both with civilian passengers and the large number of troops and munitions workers that the railways were obliged to carry. Despite the continued demand for travel facilties, a demand the government did its best to curtail, the total number of train services was drastically reduced. Competing trains on the main lines were eliminated and many connecting branch services withdrawn. Little used stations and even whole branch lines were closed in an attempt to effect economies in manpower, rolling stock and fuel. Overall there was probably a forty per cent reduction in the number of passenger trains run.[45]

The railways faced serious problems in the aftermath of war, not least the shortages of locomotives and rolling stock and the run-down state of track and equipment. It was not until the winter of 1921 that the companies made any serious attempts to restore pre-war standards of speed. A survey of express train services between London and thirty six towns by the *Railway Magazine* revealed that over half of them had services as fast or faster than those in operation during 1913–14.[46] There were also some new initiatives in long-distance cross country services at this time. Most notable perhaps was the Aberdeen to Penzance service. Routed via York, Banbury and Oxford, the train took nearly 24 hours to cover the 785 miles between Aberdeen and Penzance.

By this time the days of the independent companies were numbered. The Aberdeen–Penzance service, operated by the future eastern group and the GWR, foreshadowed the notion of greater coordination of railway services which it was hoped would be engendered by the Grouping.[47] In the early days of the groups this was still a long way off. The groups themselves still had to be moulded into workable units. Until coherent passenger policies emerged spectacular improvements in train services were unlikely. On the LMS in particular the 1920s saw few advances in express train standards as the former motive power departments of its constituents (the LYR, LNWR and Midland) vied with each other for supremacy in the new organisation. On the Southern Railway the legacy from the pre-grouping era lacked any really powerful express locomotives. Both the GWR and LNER were, perhaps, better placed in this respect, but there were still obstacles to progress.

With competition still a major fact of railway life after grouping the companies were conscious that any decision to provide faster main line trains could result in the onset of major and, from the point of view of operating economies, self-defeating competitive battles for long-distance passenger traffic. Agreements not to compete on speed ensured that overall the 1920s saw few sustained efforts in this direction, despite growing public demand for faster services. There were exceptions – notably the GWR's 'Cheltenham Flyer' introduced in 1923 – but on the whole the companies tended to concentrate on providing longer non-stop runs until, by the later 1920s, the possibilities in this direction had been more or less exhausted. Henceforth, it was only speed and/or passenger amenities which might have any serious impact on the competition for passengers.

There were also other commercial reasons behind the general lack of interest in speed standards during the 1920s. As yet the development of road transport services had made few inroads into long-distance railway traffic.[48] Nevertheless, road transport services could undercut standard fares on the railways by a considerable margin. By the mid-1920s bus/coach fares of just under 1d per mile were being offered; the equivalent ordinary third-class railway fare (fixed in 1923) was 1½d per mile and first class 2½d. Rather than speed, in which the railway was as yet unchallenged over long distances, it seemed to be fares which held the key to fending off the threat from motor transport. The result was a series of fare concessions, such as tourist, weekend and excursion tickets and the introduction of monthly returns which it was claimed allowed the passenger to travel for around 1d per mile. Whereas in 1925 the proportion of railway passenger receipts derived from reduced fares was just over 34 per cent, by 1938 it had increased to 85 per cent. In this sense the inter-war years marked the culmination of the trend towards a high volume, low margin business which had originated as far back as the mid-Victorian period. If the railways managed to hold passenger traffic at a fairly constant level between the Wars it was at the price of a steady fall in average receipts per passenger mile.[49]

Meanwhile, speed did become a more important ingredient in competition for traffic during the 1930s. Of Anglo-Scottish traffic, for example, it has been observed that competition 'remained as strong as ever – in some respects hotting up in the mid-30s.'[50] Having sorted out its motive power requirements the LMS began a series of improvements in the early 1930s. Average journey times from London to Manchester/Glasgow were significantly reduced (although best times were not significantly faster than 1913). Later the LNER captured attention with its streamlined services from King's Cross to the North commencing with the Silver Jubilee in 1935. Not to be outshone the GWR, with its Bristolian introduced the same year, offered passengers to Bristol and the West accelerated services. Other highlights of these years included named services like the West Riding Limited (King's Cross to Leeds/Braford), the Coronation (King's Cross to Edinburgh) and the Coronation Scot (Euston to Glasgow). There were also the one-off performance specials such as the GWR's Tregenna Castle run in 1932 – the fastest ever start to stop speed by steam (an average of 71.4mph) – and the LNER's Mallard run in 1938 which, with a top speed of 126mph, captured the world record for highest speed by steam.

The accelerations of the 1930s saw some worthwhile improvements in general speed standards, with even the mundane main line services showing significant reductions in journey times over the pre-war period. The major reservation was that the improvements were confined almost exclusively to the radial routes out of London. Cross-country services did not benefit to anything like the same extent. Nonetheless, these services at least benefitted from the inter-availability of ticket facilities. Under an agreement of 1933 passengers holding return tickets issued by the LMS, LNER or GWR were able to return by any recognised alternative route.[51]

Complementing these changes were improvements in carriage

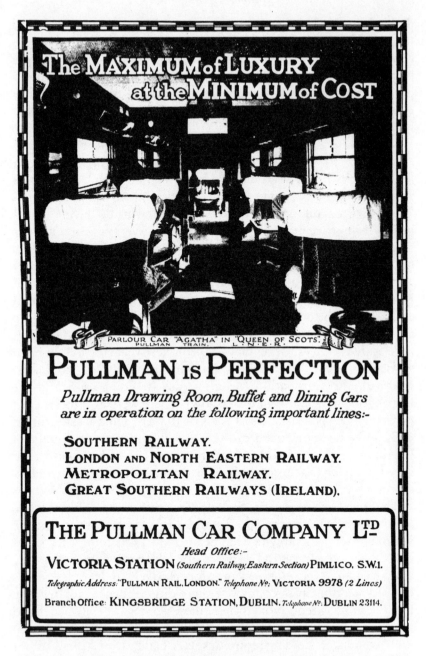

The Pullman concept of luxury railway travel as it had developed by the Inter-War period (by permission of the British Railways Board).

designs and amenities: low density seating, armchair saloons, cocktail bars, hairdressing salons, personal radio headphones and even cinema coaches were introduced on selected routes during these years. However, these facilities were of limited availability, normally reserved for first-class or Pullman passengers. Third-class passengers meanwhile still had to endure fairly basic facilities – four-a-side seating on the GWR and SR (three on some LMS and LNER trains). Perhaps the most important breakthrough for these passengers was the introduction of third-class sleeping cars following an agreement between the GWR, LMS and LNER in 1928. It was surely one of the LNER's most parsimonious decisions to supply the lavatories of these and other long-distance third-class trains with used soap from first-class sleeping cars.[52]

Overall the passenger policies of the companies between the wars were rather conservative and improvement steady rather than spectacular. The more notable developments in services and facilities were on the whole accommodated without wholesale restructuring of timetables or existing services. This sometimes had adverse effects on train punctuality. Moreover, on certain routes, particularly on Summer Saturdays and at peak periods, the general increase in long-distance traffic which marked the inter-war period regularly caused trains to be longer and heavier, again with adverse effects on punctuality.

With the exception of the Southern, the railways eschewed alternative forms of traction in favour of the proven technology of the steam locomotive. In 1931 the Weir Committee had reported in favour of main line electrification. The option was certainly not rejected outright. The SR was already committed to further electrification, albeit on the third-rail system rather than the overhead system favoured by Weir. The GWR went so far as to prepare a detailed scheme before rejecting it on the grounds of cost. The latter was the major obstacle to implementation of electrification even on suburban lines, it being by no means clear that it would have paid the companies to modernise their traction. Steam remained a known quantity and was, as the railways undoubtedly demonstrated, capable of further refinement and improved performance. By the outbreak of the Second World War, therefore, the long-distance passenger probably enjoyed 'a level of service that represented the best that could be achieved with steam traction as regards speed, frequency and comfort.'[53] It was not until after the emergence of reasonably reliable modern traction and the forging of the Inter-City network from the mid-1960s that the main line passenger began to enjoy significantly advanced standards of speed, frequency and comfort on an expanding range of long-distance services.

4
The Railway in the Countryside: The Development of Local Passenger Services

Nothing in the world can be more exhilarating than locomotion on an established railroad; but of all travelling, that on a branch line is the most irksome.

Sir George Head, 1835

The closure of large sections of the British railway network during the 1960s fell heavily on what was once an extensive system of rural railways. On the main lines hundreds of small stations which were once important centres of village life have disappeared, while the few rural branch lines that remain are often little more than elongated sidings – basic railways in current phraseology – devoid of the character and interest created by that rich mixture of peaceful countryside, steam engines, varied rolling stock, ornate station buildings, signal boxes, signals and other railway paraphenalia which make their memory such an enduring one. Not surprisingly, evocative memoirs of this arcadian image of the railway in the countryside have carved a significant niche in the recent literature of railways.[1]

But in the nineteenth century and for much of the twentieth, country railway stations and the services they offered to passengers in rural communities were much more than simply a remnant of some arcadian past: they were the very embodiment of social and economic change. As one historian of the English country railway has observed: 'The station was the place where the railway greeted its local customers and took their money, the doorway through which important people right up to royalty would pass on visits to the district ... the place where every piece of invention of the Victorian age could first be seen – from the railway's own telegraph instrument and signalling system, newest engine or crane, to threshing machines, mangles, toilet cisterns and bicycles.'[2]

Yet the influence the railway had on country towns, villages and

71

hamlets, on what one social historian terms 'the face and pace of the countryside', is difficult to assess. As Jack Simmons has argued in his invaluable survey of the railway's relationship with Victorian communities in both town and country, the railway was certainly 'an agent of change', but such was the diversity of experience in the wake of railway construction that generalisation on the quantity and quality of change is difficult and probably unwise.[3] If the answers are often tentative or incomplete the relationship between railway and passenger in the rural environment is no less worthy of exploration than in the urban. Here, then, we draw on the pioneering work of Simmons and others who have begun the long process of attempting to understand the part played by the railways in rural life. Specifically, the emphasis is on the local passenger services offered to the rural traveller: how much they were used, by whom and with what effects. To begin with though it is necessary to say something about what is meant by the term 'country' or 'rural' railway.

The Rural Railway Network

By the Edwardian age the countryside of Britain was criss-crossed by an extensive system of rural railways. Only a portion of that system comprised the rural railway in its ideal/typical form, the branch line. It might be convenient if we could confine our observations to such lines, but in practice there are several objections to what would be a restricted view of the rural system. In the first place, most of Britain's early railways, even the trunk routes, traversed an essentially rural landscape. The object may have been to link the major centres of population and industry, but the richness of the intervening agricultural land or the potential for mineral extraction did not go unnoticed by projectors and investors. The London & York Railway, for instance, emphasised not just its role as a direct and convenient line between Middlesex and Yorkshire but its ability to provide for the 'local convenience of the intermediate districts'.[4] Like the London & York, most lines served a string of small and, previously perhaps, isolated settlements along their route, and even if they failed to provide a station from the start they were always susceptible to local pressure to do so later.[5]

In another sense too, it would be misleading to rely on the branch railway as an adequate description of the rural railway. Many branches originally opened as short spurs off the main line, rapidly changed their character as they developed into important arteries of the railway system. Thus, the Wigan Branch Railway, experience of which inspired Sir George Head's deflammatory comment on the rigours of branch line travel, began life as a seven mile line pushing northwards from the Liverpool & Manchester at Parkside.[6] Later, as part of the North Union Railway, it became an important link in the West Coast route to Scotland.

Conversely, some lines with grandiose aims of forming important through routes never fulfilled their ambitions. The Bishops Castle Railway which struck out from Craven Arms on the Hereford to Shrewsbury line towards the Welsh border fell clearly into this category. Intended as the first stage in a grand through route into mid-Wales only a fraction of the railway was built. Declared insolvent in 1866 this most bucolic of branch lines incredibly survived for nearly seventy years, during which time a passenger service of sorts continued to operate.[7] This was rather more than could be said of the Potteries, Shrewsbury & North Wales Railway. As its name implies there were pretensions of grandeur, but in the event only one section of line — Shrewsbury to Blodwell and Griggion — was built. Opened in 1866 it survived until closure in 1880. The line then lay unused until reconstructed and reopened as the Shropshire & Montgomeryshire Light Railway in 1912.

Attractive, often idiosyncratic, backwaters of the rural railway network they may have been, but lines such as these were not typical. In fact four further categories of railway can be seen to have played an important role in the countryside. Firstly, the outer sections of many suburban lines served what were essentially rural districts until well into the twentieth century. Even the Metropolitan Railway, that most suburban of suburban railways, continued to retain the air of country branch line at its extremities on the edge of the Chilterns. As we shall see in chapter 5, the opening of a station on the Metropolitan or elsewhere did not automatically transform every village or small country town into burgeoning railway suburb.

Far removed from nascent suburbia, in mid- and West Wales, the far North of Scotland, parts of the West Country and East Anglia,

RAILWAY EXCURSION
TO RUFFORD,

FROM

THE TEMPERANCE
INSTITUTE AND READING ROOM,
The ELMS, Peel-street, Toxteth Park.

A PUBLIC MEETING is held, or a LECTURE (generally free) delivered, every Tuesday Evening, commencing at Half-past Seven o'clock. At the commencement of January, April, July, and October, a TEA PARTY is held, commencing at Quarter-past Six o'clock; Tickets, to Members, 6d. (who pay 1d. per week for the privileges of the room): to Non-Members, 9d.

BOOKS LENT OUT OF THE LIBRARY, to Members, every Friday Evening, at Half-past Seven o'clock.

There is also a SAVINGS' FUND where the smallest deposits are received on Tuesday and Friday Evenings.

The Room is open from Five to Nine every Evening.

ARRANGEMENTS for the day of Excursion.

On Arriving at Rufford, a Procession will be formed through the Village to the School Room, where there will be Addresses, Recitations, &c., until Twelve o'clock, when Friends from Preston will arrive, the company will then proceed to the Park of Sir T. G. Hesketh, kindly allowed by him to the visitors, where it is hoped the strictest order will be kept; after enjoying themselves in the Park, the company will return to the School Room, when other Addresses, &c., will be given.

Tea will be ready at Three o'clock, but as all cannot be accommodated at once, Twenty Minutes will be allowed each party after taking their seats.

Parties are requested not to press to the Tea, as there will be sufficient for the last.

All parties will have to show their Railway Ticket when returning to the Train.

REFRESHMENTS may be had through the day in Mr. E. Bridge's Barn.

No person intoxicated will be allowed to return by the Train.

The railway serves the cause of temperance. 'No person intoxicated' was to be allowed to return on this excursion to Rufford (from the John Johnson Collection, Railways Box 1, by permission of the Bodleian Library).

quite extensive rural networks were built and here we may identify a second, quite different, type of rural railway. These lines were evidence that neither sparseness of population nor difficulty of terrain were obstacles to the Victorian railway builders. Several of them were not branches in the conventional sense. The Cambrian Railway's line from Whitchurch to Aberyswyth, the Highland Railway's lines from Inverness to Wick, Thurso and the Kyle of Lochalsh, or the western extremities of the LSWR's and GWR's lines in Devon and Cornwall were, to the districts they served, 'main lines' – essential links with the rest of the railway network and the country as a whole.

Like these railways, the third category of rural line – the cross country railway – was also more akin to secondary main line than a country branch. The line from Newark to Market Harborough serves as one example. Built by agreement between the LNWR and GNR, this railway made possible a range of useful through journeys, especially from the East Midlands to the Lincolnshire coast. Yet the line was essentially rural in character, serving the needs of a string of remote agricultural districts. The same was true of that most individual of cross country lines – the Somerset & Dorset. Originally an independent company but later jointly owned by the LSWR and Midland, this line linked Bath and Broadstone with the small communities of Radstock, Evercreech, Templecombe, Blandford and, by a long branch, Glastonbury, Highbridge and Burnham-on-Sea. But the line became familiar to generations of holidaymakers travelling from the North and Midlands to the South coast – from the start of passenger operations two of the four daily trains included carriages from Birmingham to Bournemouth.

The final variant of rural railway – the light railway – forms almost a sub-class of the branch line. In thinly populated agricultural districts where traffic was always likely to be light and highly seasonal, such railways offered several potential advantages. Lighter axle loads and restricted speeds (eight tons and 25mph after the Regulation of Railways Act, 1868) offered the prospect of lower construction costs. But whereas in France and Belgium light railways were built in large numbers, in Britain progress was slow. It was not until relatively late in the nineteenth century that they began to be looked at seriously: in 1895 the Lord's Select

Committee on Distress from the Want of Employment advocated their construction as a means of stimulating recovery in districts hard hit by agricultural depression.

Under pressure from agricultural and light railway interests parliament passed the Light Railway Act in 1896. Under this it was possible to obtain a construction Order from the Light Railway Commissioners more cheaply than from parliament, while it also enabled local authorities to make loans and grants to light railway projects. If the Act was not the immediate success anticipated it was not the abject failure sometimes suggested. It certainly encouraged applications to build – some 700 over the next twenty five years. By 1918 over 2,000 miles of light railways had been authorised, but only 900 miles had actually been constructed. The main deficiency of the Act was that it left undisturbed the principle that railways should conform to market forces and pay their way even though they were intended to fulfil the social needs of depressed districts. With private enterprise in charge, the development of a comprehensive system was 'largely stifled by demands of profit and convenience to the promoters.'[8]

There were exceptions: in several districts light railways did much to serve local communities, their shoestring existence producing railways of individual character. One of the best known exponents of light railway 'theory' was Holman Fred Stephens. A specialist in the construction, acquisition and control of light railways, by 1916 Stephens was involved directly with seven concerns and indirectly with several others. His forte was the rescue of seemingly doomed projects. Through a combination of economy of construction and operation – light track, steep gradients, second-hand locomotives and rolling stock, the use of purpose built railbuses – he managed to keep lines such as the Kent & East Sussex (the Farmers' Line), the Bere Alston & Calstock and the Shropshire and Montgomeryshire alive. But, as with most light railways, bankruptcy was never far away. For most salvation came with amalgamation into one of the main line companies, although Stephens' lines maintained their independence until his death in 1931.[9]

Britain's rural railway network was, then, a diverse collection of types: cross country, suburban, light, narrow, and even main lines came together to serve the countryside. Passenger travel to the remoter corners of the network was never particularly quick or easy, but it was a considerable improvement on what had gone before. The diversity of the rural system makes it difficult to generalise about the services the railways offered to passengers and their impact on local communities. However, some indication of the variation in experience can be made by reference to the motives that lay behind the creation of the rural system, even though the factors behind the promotion of an important cross-country route were apt to be different from those that inspired the building of a short branch line.

Motives for Construction

By the 1860s it was generally recognised that rural districts were unlikely to yield more than a limited passenger traffic. Yet in subsequent decades railway construction consisted largely of additions to the rural network, most of it inspired, as it always had been, by the lure of profit. However, it was not always the expectation of profit from the operation of local passenger services which induced promoters to get involved in such schemes. Many of the most 'rural' of railways crossing windswept moorland, or mile after mile of sparsely populated farmland served at some point quite large communities – perhaps a seaside resort or port. Others existed primarily to serve the needs of quarrying or mining – those of North Wales and Cumberland/Westmorland for instance. Often it might be the hope of making a profit indirectly. 'The local gentlemen behind the Bedale & Leyburn', observed H. W. Parris in his important study of the Northallerton to Hawes branch, 'sold land, or lent money, to the company, and no doubt hoped for higher rents and better access to markets from it.'[10]

Profit was also the motive behind the construction of so-called contractors' lines. Anxious to keep large workforces and equipment moving from one project to another, some contractors were prepared to invest in a project on condition they received the contract for its construction. Once built their interest might wane although the practice of taking payment partly in the form of shares often ensured a continued interest even to the point of actually operating the line for a period.[11] Some of the leading contractors, notably Thomas Brassey and Samuel Morten Peto, fell into this category. Indeed Peto considered himself something of a specialist in the rural railway. Taking his cue from a report of the Belgian government on the importance of railways in rural districts, he had stated to a Select Committee in 1846 his belief that the number of people likely to travel in proportion to the total population was higher in agricultural than manufacturing districts.[12] Certainly it would be a mistake to assume that all rural lines were built only when the large inter-urban projects had been completed. Suffolk's railways, for example, were promoted and built between the 1840s and 1860s – well before the classic phase of branch line activity of the later Victorian period.

However, much of the rural railway network, particularly that part of it built during the last quarter of the century, had little chance of commercial success. Many lines survived only because they were swallowed into the systems of the large main line companies, their operating costs subsidised by the profitable sections of the business. In some cases the large companies built or acquired rural lines mainly with the intention of closing off a piece of territory from rival companies, effectively subsidising their services in return for the tactical advantages gained.[13]

The rural railway built solely as a form of public service was rare. Some, it is true, were built because a local dignatory decided to finance the project. But in such cases the boundaries between personal gain, enhanced local prestige and altruism were often obscure. Thus, the Blenheim & Woodstock branch in Oxfordshire, opened in 1890, was built by the Duke of Marlborough for the 'public and local advantage' of *both* Palace and Woodstock. Similarly, the Brill branch of the Metropolitan Railway had originally been built by the Duke of Buckingham in 1870 to carry agricultural produce and estate workers. It was only later that a public passenger service was provided, a service which survived just long enough to pass into the control of London Transport before closure of the line in 1935.[14]

Railways and Rural Life

Having briefly explored the reasons for the building of the rural network we can now turn to the railway's relationship with the rural passenger and its impact on the countryside. In an extensive study of the railway's role in the development of the mid-Victorian economy, G. R. Hawke has helped to dispel the popular notion that the railway was indispensible to the growth of the agricultural sector.[15] Certainly during 1840–70 agriculture provided only a relatively small proportion of the railway's total freight. The savings brought by the railway were more impressive in some sectors than others – in the transportation of minerals, for instance, much more than agricultural produce. While there is little doubt that the railway improved access to established markets and helped to establish new ones, it was not until later in the century that the speed advantages of the railway became 'a necessary condition for many of the developments which occurred in agriculture.'[16] In several parts of Britain such were the physical difficulties of farming or the strength of attachment to existing markets that the railway brought no obvious change to traditional farming methods. In the remoter parts of Wales, for example, one study has shown that fears of higher rents made some farmers reluctant to exploit the new marketing opportunities opened up by the railway.[17]

However, scepticism about the extent of the railway's contribution to the economy should not obscure the important changes that did take place in the countryside. As well as offering an important consumer service the railway brought an extensive source of employment. Recent research into the work and lives of railway 'navvies' has shown that the majority were drawn from the ranks of agricultural labour: local men in most instances, drawn into the work by the building of a railway through their own neighbourhoods. The L&BR, for instance, attracted labour from most of the counties along its route; the SER employed mainly local Kentish workers; the LBSC and LSWR drew labour from Sussex; the Eastern Counties Railway from Essex.[18]

Once built the railways drew a large proportion of their operating staff from the localities they served. Despite the dangers and hardships of railway service the attractions of regular work and higher wages were considerable, especially in comparison to the seasonality and poverty associated with agricultural labour. In addition, the various railway towns such as Crewe, Swindon, Wolverton, Ashford, and a host of smaller communities which grew to service the construction and repair requirements of the industry, also drew labour from the surrounding countryside. As one railway leader commented in 1884; 'All the employees that I have to deal with come mainly from the agricultural side. . . . The country feeds the towns as regards our labourers.'[19]

As the railway began to reach out across the countryside so it began to have an influence on the movement and distribution of the population. The process of rural-urban migration was, of course, already well under way before the building of railways. It seems that most migration took place over short distances, people tending to move initially to local communities where they might sample something of the culture to be found in larger urban/industrial centres.[20] How much the railway contributed to this process is difficult to assess. There is still much in the comment of one early student of migration that it is superficial to attribute the exodus from the countryside 'solely to the neighbourhood of the railways and the pleasures of the great towns.'[21] However, it is reasonable to assume that the railway simplified and, above all, reduced the cost of travel. Together with the electric telegraph, it aided the spread of information – vital to improving access to and knowledge about employment opportunities elsewhere.

Yet the obstacles to and pitfalls of migration were formidable. Ignorance of the wider world and illiteracy might pose serious problems even before the would-be migrant boarded the train. Canon Girdlestone's efforts to assist poor migrants from rural north Devon illustrate some of the difficulties:

> Almost everything had to be done for them, their luggage addressed, their railway tickets taken, and full and plain directions given . . . written on a piece of paper in a large and reliable hand. These were shown to the officials of the several lines of railway. Many of the peasants of north Devon were so ignorant of the whereabouts of the places to which they were about to be sent (in Kent and the northern counties), that they asked whether they were going 'over the water'.[22]

There were other problems. Labour markets remained very localised throughout the nineteenth century, a point true even of the major urban centres.[23] Often information on the availability of work might be spurious, workers arriving off the train to find that they had been brought to act as strikebreakers in some acrimonious industrial dispute. This happened to a group of men from the Bristol area who claimed they had been 'cruelly deceived' into travelling to Liverpool to break a strike of dockers in 1879. Some refused to work, receiving a contribution from the strikers towards their return train fare.[24] In other cases agricultural workers were tempted to migrate by unscrupulous employers anxious to tap the large reservoir of cheap rural labour. Many of the jobs, especially in the expanding urban transport trades, were casualised, relatively poorly paid with a high turnover of labour and offered the migrant neither regularity nor security of employment. Few were as fortunate as David Brindley who, having moved from rural Staffordshire to Liverpool in 1881, secured a job as railway porter at the Canada Dock goods station of the LNWR. With the relative security of this job and the added benefit of cheap railway passes from his employer, Brindley was made able to indulge in frequent travel to visit his relatives in Staffordshire.[25]

Of the impact of the railway on the populations of the country districts and communities it served it is difficult to be precise. In his early study of labour migration Redford argued that villages with a railway station increased their population.[26] A recent study of the rural Pennine communities served by the Settle & Carlisle Railway provides some evidence to support this view. Overall the population of the district served by the S&CR declined by over 8,000 between 1861 and 1911. But this disguises considerable variations between parishes. Hellifield, location of an important junction station and locomotive depot, experienced an increase in population of 200 per cent. In some contrast the remote village of Hillbeck lost 66 per cent of its population. It seems that parishes whose population were growing (or only declining marginally) contained a higher proportion of railway stations than those with a high rate of population decline. On this basis the author of the study has argued that the presence of the Settle & Carlisle line may well have played 'a vital role in the development (or at least lack of decline) of the district.'[27]

Until there are many more local studies of this kind wider assertions about the relationship between railways and population during this important period of labour movement from countryside to town will continue to lack detailed evidence to support them. While it is reasonable to suggest that in the country towns and villages it served the railway generally made some contribution to population growth, it cannot be assumed that this was so in every case. As Simmons' detailed survey has shown, some small communities that gained a railway subsequently shrank in size, while some of those that failed to secure a place on the railway map 'lost less from the deficiency than might be supposed'. Indeed, of the smaller country towns, he assures us, 'their populations rose and fell, very often as it seems without reference to railways at all.'[28]

However, as an agent of change in other aspects of country life the railway was certainly important, although the speed of change and its impact is often difficult to determine with any precision. The railway, together with improved postal services and the electric telegraph, was vital to the breakdown of rural isolation. The growing popularity of national newspapers (and national advertising), the tendency towards reporting national events in local newspapers, the decline of local time in favour of Greenwich or 'railway' time, the spread of ideas and the latest fashions: each owed much to the railway's contribution to improved communication and distribution. Gradually the country population was exposed to the same sorts of influences and given access to the same services as the urban. Even village sports were not immune to outside influences. It was largely due to the railway, for example, that local cricket customs were replaced by 'national' or MCC rules towards the end of the Victorian period.[29]

Yet in many areas of the country the decline of rural isolation was as slow as it was uneven. Despite the advent of railway communication a relatively small percentage of small communities could boast their own station. In Leicestershire as few as ten per cent of villages were connected to the railway network; in remoter counties – Westmorland and Dorset for instance – the percentage was much lower. Over large areas of the country, therefore, road transport and local carrying services continued to provide an essential link between town and countryside, consumer and market. The village carrier remained for many country people their principal source of contact with the outside world. According to one study of his role during the Victorian age the carrier continued to act as 'a kind of primitive country bus, often a mere cart, conveying the village folk, especially women and children, to the local town on market day ... [and] ... as shopping agents, purchasing goods ordered by villagers who did not wish to visit the

NOTICES.

SHORT PARTICULARS OF OFFENCES FOR WHICH PENALTIES ARE IMPOSED BY ACTS OF PARLIAMENT RELATING TO A RAILWAY COMPANY.

1. Under the provisions of the 109th Section of the Railways Clauses Consolidation Act 1845, as extended by the 7th Section of the Regulation of Railways Act 1889, any person offending against any Bye-law of the Company made for any of the above-mentioned purposes shall forfeit any sum not exceeding £5, imposed by the Company in their Bye-laws as the penalty, and if the infraction or non-observance of any such Bye-law be attended with danger or annoyance to the public or hindrance to the Company, the Company may without prejudice to any such penalty summarily interfere to obviate or remove such danger, annoyance or hindrance.

PUNISHMENT FOR OBSTRUCTING OFFICERS OF COMPANY.

2. Under the provisions of the 16th Section of the Railway Regulation Act 1840, any person wilfully obstructing or impeding the Company's officers or agents in the execution of their duty is liable to be apprehended, detained and fined Five Pounds, with two months' imprisonment in default of payment.

LEVEL CROSSING GATES.

3. Under the provisions of the 75th Section of the Railways Clauses Consolidation Act 1845, any person omitting to shut and fasten any gate set up at either side of the railways for the accommodation of the owners or occupiers of adjoining lands, after passing through the same, is liable in a penalty not exceeding Forty Shillings.

MIS-DECLARATION OF GOODS.

4. Every owner or person having the care of any carriage or goods upon the railway is by the Railways Clauses Consolidation Act, 1845, as amended by the Railways Act, 1921, required on demand to give to the collector of tolls, rates or charges, an exact account in writing signed by him giving the full name and address of the Consignee and such particulars of the nature, weight (inclusive of packing), and number of parcels or articles of merchandise handed to the Company for conveyance as may be necessary to enable the Company to calculate the charges therefor and of the point on the railway from which such carriage or goods have been set out or are about to set out and at what point the same are intended to be unloaded or taken off the railway: and if the goods conveyed by any such carriage, or brought for conveyance, be liable to the payment of different tolls, rates or charges, then such owner or other person shall specify the respective numbers or quantities thereof liable to each or any of such tolls, rates or charges. If any such owner or other person fail to give such account or to produce his waybill, or bill of lading, to such collector or other officer or servant of the Company demanding the same, or if he give a false account, or if he unload, or take off any part of his lading, or goods at any other place than shall be mentioned in such account, with intent to avoid the payment of any tolls, rates or charges payable in respect thereof, he shall for every such offence forfeit to the Company a sum not exceeding Ten Pounds for every ton of goods, or for any parcel not exceeding 1 cwt., and so in proportion for any less quantity of goods than 1 ton or for any parcel exceeding 1 cwt. (as the case may be) which shall be upon any such carriage: and such penalty shall be in addition to the toll rate or charge to which such goods may be liable.

SENDING DANGEROUS GOODS.

5. Under the provisions of the 105th Section of the same Act, no person shall be entitled to carry or to require the Company to carry on the Railway any aquafortis, oil of vitriol, gunpowder, lucifer matches, or other goods which in the judgment of the Company may be of a dangerous nature; and any person who sends by the Railway any such goods without distinctly marking their nature on the outside of the package, or otherwise giving notice in writing to the bookkeeper or servant of the Company with whom the same are left at the time of so sending, shall forfeit to the Company Twenty Pounds for every such offence. The Company are also entitled to refuse to take any parcel that they may suspect to contain goods of a dangerous nature, or to require it to be opened to ascertain the fact.

INJURING NOTICE BOARDS, &c.

6. Under the provisions of the 146th Section of the Companies' Clauses Consolidation Act 1845 or the 144th Section of the Railways Clauses Consolidation Act 1845, any person who pulls down or injures any board put up or affixed for the purpose of publishing any Bye-law or penalty, or obliterates any letter or figure thereon, shall be liable to forfeit Five Pounds and to defray the expenses of the restoration of such board.

7. Under the provisions of the 95th Section of the Railways Clauses Consolidation Act 1845 any person wilfully pulling down, defacing, or destroying any Toll Board, or Milestone, is liable in a penalty not exceeding Five Pounds, in addition to making good the damage.

DAMAGE TO PROPERTY TO BE MADE GOOD IN ADDITION TO PENALTY.

8. The 152nd Section of the Railways Clauses Consolidation Act 1845 also provides that if through any act, neglect, or default on account whereof a penalty is imposed by that or the special Act the Company's property shall have been damaged, the offenders shall be liable to make good such damage as well as to pay such penalty.

USING COMMUNICATION BETWEEN PASSENGERS AND SERVANTS OF THE COMPANY.

9. Under the provisions of the 22nd Section of the Regulation of Railways Act 1868, any Passenger who, without reasonable and sufficient cause, makes use of the means of communication between the Passengers and the Company's servants in charge of a train is liable to a penalty of Five Pounds.

PENALTY FOR TRAVELLING BEYOND STATION TO WHICH FARE PAID.

10. Under the provisions of the 103rd and 104th Sections of the Railways Clauses Consolidation Act 1845, any person who knowingly and wilfully refuses or neglects, on arriving at the point to which he has paid his fare, to quit any railway carriage is liable to a penalty of Forty Shillings.

PENALTY FOR FAILING TO PRODUCE OR DELIVER UP TICKET OR GIVE NAME AND ADDRESS.

11. By the Regulation of Railways Act 1889, every Passenger is required, on request by an officer or servant of the Company, either to produce, and if so requested to deliver up, a ticket showing that his fare is paid, or pay his fare from the place whence he started, or give such officer or servant his name and address: and every Passenger making default is subject to a fine of Forty Shillings.

DETENTION OF OFFENDERS.

12. Under the provisions of the same Act, if a Passenger, having failed either to produce or, if requested, to deliver up a ticket showing that his fare is paid, or to pay his fare, refuses on request by an officer or servant of the Company to give his name and address, he may be detained by any officer of the Company or any constable until he can be conveniently brought before some Justice.

PENALTY FOR AVOIDING PAYMENT OF FARE OR GIVING FALSE NAME OR ADDRESS.

13. Under the provisions of the same Act, any person who travels or attempts to travel on the railway without having previously paid his fare and with intent to avoid payment thereof, or who, having paid his fare for a certain distance, knowingly and wilfully proceeds by train beyond that distance without previously paying the additional fare for the additional distance, and with intent to avoid payment thereof, or who, having failed to pay his fare, gives in reply to a request by an officer of the Company a false name or address, is liable, without prejudice to recovery of the fare payable to the Company, to a fine of Forty Shillings, or, in case of a second or subsequent offence, to a fine of Twenty Pounds or a month's imprisonment.

TRESPASSING ON RAILWAY.

14. Under the provisions of the 23rd Section of the Regulation of Railways Act 1868 as amended by the 14th Section of the Regulation of Railways Act 1871, any person who shall be or pass upon the Railway except for the purpose of crossing at an authorised crossing, after having once received warning by the Company which works the Railway or by any of their agents or servants not to go or pass thereon, shall be liable to a penalty of Forty Shillings.

TRESPASSING ON RAILWAY OR STATIONS, &c.

15. Persons trespassing upon the Railways belonging to, or leased or worked by the London Midland and Scottish Railway Company or by that Company and any other Company and any persons trespassing upon the stations, works, lands or property connected with such Railways, are liable to a penalty of Forty Shillings, under the London and North Western Railway (Additional Powers) Act 1883, the Lancashire and Yorkshire Railway Act 1884, the Glasgow and South Western Railway (Additional Powers) Act 1892, and the Caledonian Railway Act 1898, or to a penalty of Ten Pounds under the Midland Railway Consolidation Act 1844; and in accordance with the provisions of the said Acts public warning is hereby given to all persons not to trespass upon the said Railways, stations, works, lands or property.

16. Under the provisions of the 48th Section of the Lancashire and Yorkshire Railway Act 1913, any person who shall be found sleeping or lodging without reasonable excuse in any Railway carriage standing on any siding or standage line of the Company, or shall commit any nuisance or act of indecency in any such carriage shall be liable on conviction to a penalty not exceeding Forty Shillings.

For so public an industry as the railways a legal 'framework' governing the relationship with passengers (and other railway users) was indispensable. This litany of offences and penalties appeared in the LMS timetable of 1939.

town themselves, or were unable to do so.'[30]

While large sections of the competitive transport system were killed off by the railways, it is evident that a complementary system survived, even prospered, with road transport services in particular playing a vital local feeder and distribution role to the railway.[31] This was true even of those villages with ostensibly their own station. Although the railway companies paid considerable attention to the siting of their stations, not infrequently they were some distance from the village of the same name. Even light railways could fall into this trap: the Basingstoke & Alton's intermediate stations were all a mile or so from the nearest village. The necessity for connecting road services of some kind is readily apparent, as is the susceptibility of the railway to competition from the motor vehicle in a later age.

This is not to deny that the rural railway played an important role in serving the countryside. The stations, as we have seen, often acted as focal points of community life. Unfortunately, the use made of the passenger services offered by the railways is now difficult to reconstruct because so few records of traffic along individual lines have survived. However, one study of the surviving records of stations along the Midland Railway's Settle & Carlisle line has revealed an interesting picture of local traffic patterns. The majority of passengers seem to have used the line to visit a neighbouring community rather than travelling further afield. Principal destinations, not surprisingly, were the major market or administrative centres such as Settle, Appleby and Carlisle itself, and to a lesser extent, Kirby Stephen and Hawes. A significant number of passengers from the southern end of the line travelled beyond Settle particularly to Skipton. The main conclusion of the study is that the railway was used 'almost exclusively as a local amenity rather than as a means of leaving the area.'[32]

As to the precise reasons for making local journeys, whether on the Settle & Carlisle or elsewhere, there is little direct evidence. Peto, who as we have seen was adamant that country people were extensive railway travellers, was rather vague in explaining why. There seems little reason to suppose that the agricultural labourer had any more reason to travel on a daily basis than his counterpart in the town. Nor, of course, would he have had the wherewithal to do so. However, rural lines would have been used on a more regular basis by farmers and others with interests in agricultural business travelling to the various markets around the country. The number of these markets and their associated fairs declined considerably with the coming of the railway, their survival depending largely on access by train. By 1888 no less than 390 of the 420 surviving markets had a railway station in close proximity.[33]

The railway also imposed changes on other aspects of agriculture. The rapid growth of livestock traffic did much to replace the old-established droving trades whereby livestock of all kinds was moved on the hoof from rearing to fattening districts and later to market. While the drover disappeared he was replaced by a new, if numerically insignificant, category of railway passenger – the grazier who travelled with his livestock on the train.[34] The market widening effects of the railway also created another type of passenger, the seasonal migrant. Expanding and diversifying demand for food from the urban areas gave farmers an incentive to expand and extend production, all of which required more not less labour. The seasonal migration of labourers, particularly at harvest periods, must have brought some additional traffic to the rural railways. Certainly gangs of Irish harvesters were carried in special trains of cattle trucks by the LNWR from Liverpool to places as far away as Rugby, Peterborough and Watford.[35] The annual hop pickers' specials from London into the Kentish countryside and elsewhere provide a further example of extra traffic arising from these changes.

Beyond this though we can only speculate on the pattern of use of rural lines. The outward flow of migrants must have constituted an important, if occasional, source of traffic. Subsequent return trips to visit kin and friends were doubtless also to the railways' advantage. Other, more regular, travel to the nearest market town for shopping, business and/or social purposes would also have been important. This would certainly conform to the pattern of use revealed in some modern surveys of passenger traffic on rural lines.[36] However, the problem facing many lines, even in the days before competition from the motor vehicle, was that while the proportion of the local population actually using their local railway could be quite high, the volume of passengers on a daily basis was still low. Put another way, local train journeys made by rural passengers were made on a fairly regular, but infrequent basis.

There is some evidence to support this view. On the Northallerton to Hawes branch the average train in 1857 carried no more than 13 or 14 passengers.[37] Along the Settle & Carlisle line the peak years of local use (1895–1905) saw nearly 150,000 passengers a year booking tickets at the various stations en route. On a daily basis this represented just 500 passengers using 20 stations and perhaps 7 trains: 'Thus, even at maximum, the average number of passengers offering themselves for each local train at any one station was less than five.'[38] Translated into receipts such low daily use often presented a dismal picture. Simmons cites the case of Chollerton on the Border Counties Railway where in 1861 and 1865 the receipts amounted to just 15s. a day.[39] If some companies, the GER for example, appear to have lived reasonably contentedly with large rural systems, invariably it was because revenue from other traffic – through passengers, suburban and freight – made it possible.

Despite some exceptions, low patronage, a spartan service of trains and meagre revenue was the all too familiar pattern of rural railway operation in Britain. Yet historians have been prevented from making anything more than impressionistic judgements about financial performance because so few records indicating the relative profitability of individual parts of the larger company systems have survived. Nor, apparently, were the companies themselves acutely sensitive to or aware of the costs of operating particular types of services. The aggregate picture of profitability in the entire organisation was what mattered most. The cost pricing policy of the companies, denigrated by one historian as 'decidedly unscientific', concentrated not on the actual costs of operation, but on 'what the traffic would bear.'[40] On the whole the companies implicitly accepted the principle of cross subsidisation, revenue from high value traffic on the more remunerative parts of the system being used to cover the losses from less remunerative parts. It is perfectly possible, therefore, that large numbers of rural railways survived for so long because, as Simmons has observed, 'no one examined, in strict accountacy, the losses they entailed.'[41]

This is one reason why the mileage of railway closed prior to the First World War was exceedingly small – perhaps a net total of 210 miles. Another was the largely unchallenged position of the railway prior to the war. In the early years of the twentieth century electric tramcar and motor omnibus services had begun to make serious inroads into the railways' established short distance traffic. After the war the rural network also began to suffer from rapid development of country bus and other road services. The surviving independent light railways found times especially difficult. Saddled with high interest charges incurred in earlier years and with little capital to invest in modern trains and equipment, several offered a decidedly inferior service to their competitors:

> An elderly 0–6–0 or tank engine, requiring constant maintenance and expensive fuel, was no match for a modern motor bus, nor could the latter's comfort be equalled by four or six wheel coaches often dating from the Victorian era.[42]

By 1939 only sixteen independent light railways had survived. Meanwhile, the rural lines of the main line companies had also suffered badly. The practice of cross-subsidisation saved many, but still over 1,000 miles of railways, predominantly rural branches, were closed between the wars. That the total was not much higher has been interpreted by some commentators as a failure by railway management to identify and eradicate what were patently uneconomic services.[43] Certainly the loss of revenue from local services due primarily to road competition could assume alarming proportions. On the LNER, for example, revenue from one local service – Middlesborough to Eston – declined by 94 per cent in the years leading up to 1927. Although an extreme case the same company experienced difficulties on a range of local services. The main responses by the railways to the problem of the rural bus were cheap fares and attempts to acquire a financial stake in the bus companies themselves, neither of which could be guaranteed to reverse either the decline in passengers or revenue.[44]

This is not the place to enter into the debate on the quality and performance of railway management between the Wars. Here the central question concerns the customer rather more than the operator: would the rural passenger have been adversely affected by the closure of a greater proportion of the network? It can be argued that replacement bus services might have served local needs more flexibly and efficiently than the railway. There were those in the industry prepared to argue that the time had come for the railways to take drastic measures. 'It is acknowledged', wrote one member of the LNER management, 'that the slow all-station services are intended to serve as feeder trains . . . but associated road services are now operated in most districts between market towns and villages and I consider the time is now opportune to take advantage of these services by eliminating as far as possible the slow train calling at each wayside station. . . . I think in practice that the passenger would prefer to travel by road service to the nearest rail centre. . . . The small wayside station has in most instances outlived its usefulness.'[45]

Although a chilling rehearsal of the arguments that accompanied the dismemberment of the rural railway network during the 1960s, these views found little support within the industry prior to the Second World War. Few were prepared, even for tactical reasons, to concede defeat to road competition except in the most hopeless of cases. It was, in any case, by no means certain, as experience was to demonstrate during the modern era of line and station closures, that rural bus services would have fared any better than the trains they replaced. The more sanguine in the bus industry were even prepared to acknowledge this point. The replacement of rail services by buses 'sounded very nice in theory', admitted the traffic manager of one Midlands bus company in 1939, 'but in practice . . . it was found that where a branch railway line had been closed down and a road service had been run, that road service had never even earned its working expenses. It would, therefore, appear that if there was not sufficient traffic for a rail service there was not sufficient traffic for a road service.'[46]

In a sense something of the spirit that had created the rural railway network lived on during the inter-war years and the system survived largely intact. Although inspired by and operated on the expectation of profit, the reality was that the railway in the countryside offered its passengers something akin to a social service. It remains something of a paradox in the relationship between railway and passenger that the crisis for most rural lines came not when their affairs were controlled by private owners, but later when, as a nationalised industry facing successive shifts in political control, railway finances were critically examined as an item of public expenditure and social policy. Then, as H. W. Parris acutely observed, the problem of branch lines in particular became not one of 'getting back to some Golden Age of prosperity, but of making them prosperous for the first time.'[47]

5
The Suburban Railway and the Commuter

The office is one thing, and private life is another. When I go into the office, I leave the Castle behind me, and when I come into the Castle, I leave the office behind me.

Charles Dickens, *Great Expectations*

The Castle to which Dickens' character Wemmick referred was a house in the London suburb of Walworth – then only a small village lying between Kennington Park, the Old Kent Road and Camberwell. The office, on the other hand, was located in Little Britain near St Paul's and to reach it involved a lengthy daily walk. Wemmick, of course, had his own reasons for wishing to remove himself from the office and his employer, Jaggers. But the desire to distance the home from the workplace was one of the characteristic features of Victorian society. The early suburbs, as Wemmick's experience suggests, developed before the provision of railway services. Their residents either walked or, if they could afford it, they travelled in by short stage coach or private carriage. The advent of horse-drawn omnibus services from the 1830s made suburban residences more accessible, although the cost of travel remained relatively high.

It was not really until the second half of the nineteenth century that the railway began to assume any real importance for the daily journey to work. In earlier days the emphasis had been on connecting the major towns. Although suburban stations were occasionally built on the main lines, their services were usually spartan and expensive. Harrow on the line from London to Birmingham was not untypical, served by only four trains a day with fares into London ranging from 2s second class to 3s 6d first. The attitude of the companies to suburban traffic was exemplified by the GWR which did not even refer to the word suburban in its timetables until the late 1860s. The Eastern Counties Railway, later (as the GER) to emerge as a specialist in suburban traffic, was also slow to adapt to the needs of suburban passengers. In 1845 *Herapath's Railway Journal,* always prepared to highlight an opportunity for increasing railway dividends, felt moved to advise the directors 'to make the neighbourhood of their line the residence of businessmen who are obliged to travel – not idle drones, who spend their time in hunting, shooting or trifling gossiping.'[1]

Although it might be reasonable to assume an expansion in the demand for railway commuter services, in absolute terms the mid-Victorian market was fairly restricted. Even in London, where 'commuting' had advanced furthest, there were by the 1850s perhaps 27,000 suburbanites arriving by train, compared to approximately 244,000 who used the omnibuses or, like Wemmick, simply walked.[2] From the perspective of the companies it was not always easy to justify committing extra resources to suburban services in anticipation of future demand. From the 1860s, however, the railways did begin to respond more energetically to the expanding demand for suburban railway services. With the bulk of the main line network already completed, construction activity increasingly focused on improving and extending the suburban lines into the major cities. At this stage, therefore, it is appropriate to survey briefly the main outlines of suburban railway development prior to the First World War.

Suburban Railways in London

The story of suburban railway development in London is long and complex and has been comprehensively treated by a number of historians.[3] Here we concentrate on the major themes in the building of the network and particularly on the two problems which arguably did most to influence the end product so far as the passenger was concerned.

The first – the question of better access to the central areas of the city – was a problem facing all railways serving the capital. The first railway into London, the London & Greenwich opened in 1838, built its terminus at London Bridge, a rather more central location than that later secured by either the London & Birmingham or GWR at Euston and Paddington respectively. Because of its convenience for the City, London Bridge station was adopted by the

London & Croydon, the London & Brighton and the South Eastern during the 1840s. On the north bank of the Thames the only station which could compete with London Bridge for access to the City was Fenchurch Street, opened in 1841 as the terminus of another local railway – the London & Blackwell. Again this was later colonised by other companies – the Eastern Counties, the LNWR and the London, Tilbury & Southend.

Because of their location, London Bridge and Fenchurch Street secured an early lead in the handling of suburban services, an advantage reinforced by the recommendation of the Royal Commission on Metropolitan Termini in 1846 that future railways should be excluded from an area of central London known as the Quadrilateral.[4] Nevertheless, growing suburban traffic ensured that the railways never gave up the fight for more central locations for their stations. This was reinforced by the second problem relating to railway development during this period, traffic congestion. As we have seen, the streets leading to the principal stations were increasingly crowded by people, carriages, cabs, omnibuses, drays and other delivery vehicles. The growth of suburban traffic – commuters arriving during the peak, wives and families travelling in off-peak attracted by the growth of retail and department stores in the West End, and tradesmen of various sorts – exacerbated traffic problems.

Two possible solutions were to emerge. South of the Thames the railways favoured the conventional approach, carrying their lines by viaducts and bridges towards more central terminal sites. During the 1850s and 1860s overground extensions to new stations at Victoria, Charing Cross, Ludgate Hill and Holborn were sanctioned. North of the Thames, the approach was less conventional – the underground railway. The first of these, the Metropolitan Railway, emerged out of a scheme for a line from King's Cross to Edgware Road which, after several setbacks, was eventually opened with much fanfare as the world's first underground railway in 1863.

Essentially a conventional steam railway in an unconventional setting the 'Drain', as the Metropolitan was popularly known, made a significant contribution to suburban travel.[5] With a financial stake in the company the GWR used the line as a means of generating traffic from as far out as Windsor. The GNR ran some services from its Hertfordshire suburbs onto Metropolitan tracks, as did the Midland, notably a fifty mile service linking Bedford, Luton, St Albans and Hendon with Moorgate Street in the City. The Metropolitan itself was committed to suburban traffic, building a new terminus at Moorgate Street and feeder branches to Hammersmith, Kensington and Swiss Cottage. Such was the growth of traffic that extra tracks were provided from King's Cross to Farrington Street and the extension to Moorgate. The 'widened lines', as they were called, also made connection near Farringdon with the London & Chatham's new surface line via Ludgate Hill and Holborn.[6]

Despite the soot and fumes the Metropolitan had little difficulty attracting passengers to its subterranean stations, its success leading to the building of other lines underneath the streets of London. It was soon followed by the Metropolitan District (South Kensington––Westminster Bridge, 1868) which, in 1884, joined with the Metropolitan to form the 'Inner Circle' – a major step in the creation of an underground 'system'. The building of the first deep-level tubes in the 1890s took this a stage further. Operated by electric traction from the start (the Metropolitan was not converted until 1905) and physically distinct from the rest of London's railways, the tube lines were to complete the outlines of the modern London railway network.

In the twentieth century the emphasis shifted from construction to improvement. Prior to 1914 this meant limited electrification and the intensification of conventional steam-hauled suburban services. These improvements were in many cases intended to counter competition for local traffic from electric tramway services. The latter expanded rapidly during these years both within and outside the municipal boundaries. South London in particular benefitted from the extension of the London County Council system especially after the completion of the first direct connections over the Thames via the Vauxhall and Westminster Bridges. The popularity of tramway services had serious consequences for the railways. As one report on London's housing and locomotion observed in 1907: 'The discontinuance of local trains, the decrease in the local assessment of railways, and the lessening of local traffic, have been among the most marked effects of the development of electric trams in South London, and all point to the future reservation of the railway for long distance and express through trains.'[7]

Perhaps this was premature. Through electrification the railways were able to effect significant improvements in the speed, intensity and comfort of local services. The underground and tube railways had shown the potential of electrification. On the District's Hounslow line, for example, the number of trains increased from 38 in 1904 (the last year of steam operation) to 90 in 1907; on the Ealing–Mill Hill Park line the increase over the same period was from 47 to 111 trains. South of the Thames the first 'surface railway' electrification projects, pioneered by the LBSC and LSWR, also brought some worthwhile improvements. On the LSWR's Wimbledon line, for instance, the faster acceleration and easier change round of the electric trains introduced in 1915 reduced the journey time from Waterloo to East Putney by 7 minutes and to Wimbledon Park by 8 minutes. Elsewhere in London steam still reigned supreme on suburban services. While faster and more intensive steam services were possible, south of the Thames at least the future for the suburban railway clearly lay with the electric train.

Suburban Railways in the Provinces

Although not on the scale of London, most Victorian cities could boast some important suburban railway services. On Merseyside suburban lines reached out from Liverpool Exchange northwards to the seaside resort cum residential town of Southport and the old market town of Ormskirk. To the south the suburbs of Aigburth and Garston were served by the line from Central, while to the east the lines towards Manchester and London had added a suburban function to their inter-city status.

Across the Mersey on the Wirral peninsula local railways were provided initially to act as feeders to the river ferries. In 1886 these lines were given a new role with the opening of the Mersey Railway under the river. Initially steam operated, this railway was a triumph of engineering but a commercial failure. Travel in the smoke filled tunnel was an unpleasant affair and the line's true potential as a suburban railway for Wirral commuters was only realised after it was electrified in 1903. Electrification was also adopted by the LYR on its lines to Southport and Ormskirk between 1904 and 1913 in part to complete with municipal electric tramways. But a pioneer in this respect was the Liverpool Overhead Railway, the world's first elevated electric railway, which fulfilled an important local role serving the entire length of Liverpool's waterfront.[8]

Apart from London and Liverpool electrified suburban railways were to be found in only two other centres – on Tyneside and, to a lesser extent, around Manchester. During the nineteenth century the lines on the north bank of the Tyne had been connected to form a circular route from Newcastle to Tynemouth and Whitley Bay returning via Gosforth. In 1904 the NER electrified the line as far as Whitley Bay in an attempt to compete with the electric tramway. South of the Tyne, however, local services remained steam-hauled.

Manchester could boast a fairly extensive collection of suburban lines, but like Tyneside the system was never developed to anything like its full potential. South of the city the lines to Crewe and Chester served the growing outer suburbs of Alderley Edge, Bowden and Altrincham and closer in at Cheadle Hulme, Wilmslow, and Sale. To the west the Warrington line served Flixton and Urmston, while to the north the Bury line was associated with the development of Crumpsall, Prestwich and Radcliffe. By the early 1900s this line was losing traffic to Manchester's expanding tramway network, prompting the company to electrify it. Opened in 1916 it remained a one-off, the LYR abandoning plans to electrify its lines to Oldham and Rochdale. Although quite extensive Manchester's suburban system was marred by the absence of any genuine cross-city links connecting the lines to the north and south of the city.[9]

The railways serving the industrial towns of the Midlands maintained some important suburban services, though not surprisingly it was Birmingham with the most developed system. The Birmingham West Suburban Railway and the lines out of New Street serving Sutton Coalfield and Harborne became important commuter routes during the 1860s and 1870s. To the south east of the city the GWR main line out of Snow Hill also carried suburban traffic to places like Solihull and Dorridge. The same company's Birmingham and North Warwickshire line, encouraged the growth of suburban traffic to Stratford, Shirley, Solihull, Knowle and other places located in Birmingham's 'Beautiful Borderlands'.[10]

Although there were several other major towns with lively

suburban services during this period, our survey would not be complete without mention of Glasgow. In the cases cited the developing suburbs acted as dormitories for a growing number of commuters whose work was located in the city centres. In Glasgow this was reversed, the city acting as the dormitory with people commuting to a range of work locations located on the fringes of city. Although the city had its 'conventional' suburban services to outlying communities – on the lines to the Ayrshire and Dumbartonshire coasts for instance – season ticket traffic was fairly slow to develop. Glasgow's limited suburban sprawl and the popularity of steamer services on the River Clyde did much to restrict the opportunities for the railways to develop more extensive suburban services.[11]

The Railways and Suburbia

As the railways completed their suburban railway projects the fringes of the urban areas and, beyond them, the villages and small towns that often formed the nucleii of the new suburbs, expanded considerably. But the development of 'suburbia', as it became known, depended on more than the railway and its new breed of passenger, the 'commuter'. The flight from the city by the better-off derived its dynamism from the powerful social and economic forces unleashed by industrialisation and the rise of a class society. The smoke, grime and noise of burgeoning industrial towns and cities; the problems of poverty, disease and crime; the competition for land and housing: these were the factors which produced the desire to find more peaceful and spacious retreats on the edge of town, or beyond in some arcadian country village. The process was not confined to the teeming cities nor did it depend on the railway. Oldham's business elite, for example, began to desert their former homes in the town centre in favour of 'large gardened mansions' on the edges of town early in the nineteenth century.[12] This was repeated on a larger scale, of course, in the major cities where, as the best authority on the subject has observed, the development of suburbs 'preceeded the provision of railway services, by periods of at least a decade or two.'[13]

Important though it was, most historians agree that the railway was not solely responsible for the creation of suburbs. The timing,

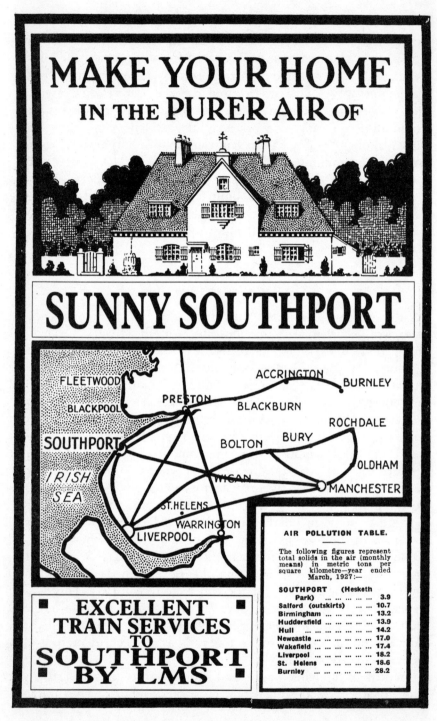

Local authority and railway company combine to promote 'Sunny Southport – England's Seaside Garden City' as 'an ideal place of residence for those who desire to separate home from business'. (By courtesy of the Tourism and Attractions Department, Sefton MBC).

location, extent and type of suburban growth might be crucially influenced by the existence of railways, but was also dependent on a range of other factors. The demand for suburban housing was affected by the level of personal incomes, new employment opportunities, the availability of credit and whether people had the time to commute. It was no coincidence that the earliest inhabitants of suburbia were drawn mainly from the middle classes, their ability to move to the suburbs facilitated, especially later in the century, by rising real incomes, the expansion of white collar occupations, reductions in hours of work, new opportunities to borrow money and a social competitiveness which expressed itself in the determination to buy the best property and most prestigious address possible.

But where, when and how much a particular suburb grew depended on other factors: the supply of building land; the attitude of landowners and established residents; and, of course, the availability of transport to the place of work in the town. The railway might act as a catalyst in bringing about suburban growth, but only in conjunction with these vital demand and supply factors. The cases of the Victorian suburbs of Hayes and Bromley illustrate the point.

In mid-Victorian years the two communities seemed to offer great potential for suburban growth. Bromley, a small town with a rural flavour, had begun to see some residential development before the arrival of the railway, but further growth was dependent on improving access to London. A station serving Bromley was opened on the Mid Kent Railway in 1858, but its location was inconvenient and the service sparse. Despite these apparent handicaps, over the next decade or so Bromley saw considerable residential development. With the high cost of commuting and the poor service seemingly not deterring would-be residents, a second railway – a branch linking Bromley with Grove Park on the SER's London–Chislehurst line opened in 1878 – confirmed the town's status as desirable railway suburb.[14]

Like Bromley the village of Hayes might have been thought to offer great potential as a future railway suburb for affluent London commuters. Various proposals were put forward to link Hayes with the railway network, but it was not until the opening of the branch line from Elmer's End by the West Wickham & Hayes Railway in

1882 that direct access to London by train became possible. Although there was every reason to expect the opening of the railway to disturb the tranquility of the large houses that dominated the district, there was remarkably little building until the 1920s. So little, in fact, that through services to London were not considered necessary until the early twentieth century.[15]

The contrasting fortunes of Bromley and Hayes suggest that the arrival of the railway might have little direct impact on the pace of suburban development. Although it was often a necessary condition for continued residential development, on its own the railway was not a sufficient cause. In the case of these communities the fortunes of the main landowners and their estate policies were instrumental. In Hayes the principal landowners not only refused to support the building of a railway, but also, until after the First World War, refused to sell off any significant parcels of land for speculative building. In Bromley, however, two large estates became available for building development as the railway arrived in the district. Thus, the acquisition of land in sufficient quantity by those 'not against development and . . . improvement minded' enabled suburban Bromley, aided by the railway, to grow so rapidly.[16]

One further example may be cited to illustrate the importance of land availability and estate policies to the development of railway suburbs. The emergence of Southport on the Lancashire coast from small 'bathing village' into a refined residential town for the well-to-do during the second half of the nineteenth century owed much to the arrival of the railway. The opening of the first railway – the Liverpool, Crosby & Southport – in 1849 soon brought reports of 'gentlemen of business, who daily visit their office in Liverpool, returning in the evening to their families located in healthy Southport.'[17] Further railways running east across the flat mosslands towards Wigan, Bolton and Manchester during the 1850s extended the possibilities of commuting. However, the scale and class of suburban development owed little to the railways. Rather it was determined largely by the policies of the town's principal landowners which had been formulated earlier in the century.

The town's principal thoroughfare – Lord Street – had been laid out as a wide and elegant boulevard during the 1820s. Planned, high class residential development undertaken primarily by the Scarisbrick and Hesketh estates followed in its wake. By leasing only large plots of land and imposing restrictions on property use and sub-letting, the intention was to attract mainly the wealthier members of the middle classes to large mansions. Although there was some tension between the needs of residents and the growing numbers who visited the town in its role as fashionable seaside resort, on the whole the use of the leasehold system secured the desired aim of avoiding 'offensive' developments. Moreover, such policies spared the landowners much expense in providing street paving and sewers. It was assumed that the type of residents attracted would have sufficient means to do this for themselves, considering it 'a small price to pay for the haven of exclusive middle class respectability.'[18]

Rather than the railway, therefore, it was landowners who did most to determine the social composition of early railway suburbs. As one historian has shown the aristocracy and gentry often aimed for the prestige end of the market – select residential areas with easy access by train to factory or office in town. Although profit was always a concern such developments also did much to 'enhance rather than debase the family's standing in the eyes of the world.'[19] Where land was held in smaller blocks by a multiplicity of owners of lower status, then the emphasis seems to have been on securing the greatest profit 'through the most intensive type of available development regardless of its social class.'[20] Such policies, combined with the determination of those who moved to the suburbs to find the best and most exclusive accommodation possible, did much to produce socially segregated communities.

But the social exclusivity of early suburbs was not immutable. For example, by the early 1900s it was observed of the suburban districts of south east London that 'neither rich nor poor predominate. . . . On the tops of the hills are the houses of the rich, while the poor live near the river plain. In Blackheath and off Shooter's Hill there are still large country-like houses with woods and pastures attached: but gradually all over the area the rich are leaving; their houses are pulled down and their gardens measured into plots for detached and semi-detached villas, or ruled into serried rows of two-storeyed houses, suitable for clerks or higher-grade artisans.'[21]

The process of suburban change is vividly described in H. J. Dyos' study of Victorian Camberwell. Originally a middle-class suburb, the district developed before the arrival of the railway. Leasehold development of high class houses set on plots of an acre or more set the social tone until mid-century. Thereafter, estates of smaller, often terraced, houses began to dominate, encouraging the 'emigration of its top people and the immigration of a different breed of newcomers from some inner suburb.'[22] From the 1870s and 1880s the morning and evening commuter trains out of Camberwell, and a host of other suburban 'transit camps' like it, began to play host to members of the lower middle classes – clerks and other white collared workers – to whom suburban living was increasingly accessible.

Included in this category were growing numbers of artisans: 'men of settled employment rather better paid', as Charles Booth described them in 1901, 'whose new homes are now being rapidly built on all sides of London, as fast as the means of communication are extended.'[23] For most the preferred means of conveyance from home to work was the tram or omnibus. However, many used the railways, often travelling on specially designated workmen's trains at cheaper fares. The development of these services and their importance to the emergence of working-class suburbs are considered in the next section.

Cheap Fares and the Working-Class Commuter

By the late Victorian period the problems of overcrowding, delapidation and decay in the residential inner districts of the major cities had become, in the words of Lord Salisbury, 'a scandal to our civilisation.' As we have seen, the building of urban railways had often aggravated the housing problem. The driving of the railway through Dickens' fictious Stagg's Gardens had disastrous consequences: 'Houses were knocked down; streets broken through and stopped; deep pits and trenches dug in the ground; enormous heaps of earth and clay thrown up; buildings that were undermined and shaking, propped by great beams of wood. . . . Everywhere were bridges that led nowhere; thoroughfares that were wholly impassable . . . carcasses of ragged tenements, and fragments of unfinished walls and arches.'[24] Having contributed to the urban housing problem the railway might have been expected, as an increasingly vocal lobby argued, to provide a solution and provide those displaced with adequate services between new areas of working-class housing in the suburbs and places of work in the city.

That the railway companies should provide a *quid pro quo* for their demolition of city dwellings was recognised in several individual Railway Acts during the 1860s. The LCDR's metropolitan extension, for example, had involved the demolition of dozens of working-class houses. As compensation the company had to accept a statutory obligation to provide cheap workmen's tickets to enable displaced families to move out while allowing the breadwinner to retain employment in town. Thus, early in 1865, the company began running workmen's trains, as they became known, between Blackfriars, Ludgate Hill and Victoria.[25] Henceforth the number of workmen's trains provided under clauses inserted in enabling Acts increased. By 1883 six companies were obliged to run eleven trains daily in the London area. By this time the majority of London companies, with the exceptions of the GWR, LNWR and Midland, ran some workmen's services even where no statutory obligation existed, providing London's earliest working-class commuters with a total of 110 trains daily.[26]

The Cheap Trains Act of 1883, as we have seen, gave to the Board of Trade powers to compel the companies to introduce concessionary fares. Yet it did not remove the voluntary provision by the companies. For example, the GER which ran 49 workmen's trains daily by 1890 was under obligation to provide only 5 trains; the LBSC was under no statutory obligation to run workmen's trains but nevertheless considered it worth its while providing 13 morning trains.[27] In the provinces too several of the companies ran a limited number of workmen's trains or offered concessionary fares on certain ordinary services, among them the LNWR in the districts of Liverpool, Manchester, Wolverhampton, Newport Pagnell and several other places; the GWR between Ffestiniog–Blaenau, Clifton Bridge–Portishead, Purton–Swindon; the NER on Tyneside and Wearside; the Caledonian and Glasgow & South Western Railways in the Glasgow area.[28]

Apologists for the railways were never slow to turn such voluntarism to political advantage. 'The railway companies', asserted the *Railway News* in 1890, 'have on the whole done far more than was required of them by Act of Parliament, and have provided, at great inconvenience to the working of their system and a minimum of profit, services of trains which have enabled the working classes to live at a distance from their work, which would otherwise be impossible.'[29] But this was only half the story. The total number of workmen's trains may have increased from 466 a day in 1897 to 1,966 in 1914, but resistance to their provision by several of the leading companies was entrenched.

In theory it would have been possible for the Board of Trade to exercise its powers to the full and compel the companies to increase the range and scope of cheap train services. But to have done so would have required more rigorous definition of what constituted a workman's train, a more searching inquiry into company accounts and much greater interference in existing traffic arrangements. In short, it would have necessitated taking responsibility for a large share of railway administration out of the hands of managers and vesting it in Whitehall bureaucrats, something the Board was extremely reluctant to embrace. In practice, therefore, the Board adopted a much less interfering role than it might have done, its policy summarised somewhat hopefully by its President, Joseph Chamberlain, in 1884: 'The evidence we have shows that we may safely rely upon the voluntary action of the Railway Companies, stimulated as it will be from time to time by a certain amount of judicious pressure.'[30]

Not that such faith impressed reformers concerned with the working-class housing problem. For example, in the early 1900s the Browning Hall Conferences on Housing and Locomotion presided over by Charles Booth and other influential civic and church leaders, condemned London's railway companies for evading their obligation to run workmen's trains: 'The routes of these railways embrace all districts, but except in a few instances do not give really efficient local services. . . . Witness the slender facilities offered by the North-Western, the Midland and the G.N.R. railways, three of our most powerful companies, and compare this with the way in which the Great Eastern deal with this class of traffic.'[31] The latter alone was praised for its cheap and frequent services, allowing workers to travel in from as far out as Walthamstow, seven miles from Liverpool Street, at fares of between 2d and 4d.

Earlier the GWR and the LNWR had been criticised by the London County Council for their failure to run any workmen's trains making it necessary for workers from Willesden, Acton and Hanwell to walk some four miles or more to a station which did issue cheap tickets.[32] Workmen living in South London were ostensibly better served, although in 1897 it was reported that of the estimated 150,000 workers needing to travel out of the district each day, less than half could find accommodation on workmen's trains.[33] In the provinces the provision for cheap railway travel was even more restricted. During the 1890s the total number of workmen's tickets issued by the three major railway companies serving Liverpool amounted to no more than 1,500 a day; in Birmingham the total was approximately the same; in Manchester somewhat higher at around 7,900 but still a small proportion of the total population of the city.[34]

There were several reasons why workmen's services did not expand as rapidly as reformers had hoped, not all of them connected with the railway companies. Those commentators, including the *Times* newspaper, who earlier in the century had claimed that by demolishing overcrowded and insanitary residential districts the railways would effectively drive the people into new and better accommodation in the suburbs, had seriously under-estimated the immobility of many workers. For the thousands of casually employed and those who needed to share tools it remained essential to live close to work. Irregular working hours and frequent enforced bouts of idleness because of seasonal or trade fluctuations made the concept of a regular morning and evening journey by train irrelevant to such workers. Social and cultural pressures reinforced the need to live in traditional areas close to work:

> Expensive meals away from home . . . the absence of cheap suburban sales of fish and meat . . . the loss of the society of friends in a community where length of residence increased the chances of help in times of trouble and the lack of congenial company and amusements, all lessened the recognised advantages of improved health and better housing in the suburbs.[35]

Nor was the development of rapid and cheap transit sufficient to attract working-class families to the suburbs. An attachment to the view that the housing problem was simply a question of time and space afflicted many, particularly those who, for ideological reasons, wished to deflect attention from the failure of market forces to provide a stock of habitable housing. 'I am quite sure', Mr Balfour assured the House of Commons in 1900, 'that . . . the great disease of overcrowding . . . can only be solved in the case of the working classes, as it has been in the case of the merchant and the clerk, by a great augmentation in the number, and a great increase in the cheapness of our methods of conveyance from one place to another.'[36] But as more percipient observers realised there had to be more to the prescription than this. The Browning Hall conferences, for instance, saw a complete system of rapid and cheap transit as only a primary step. As the Lord Provost of Glasgow observed: 'If you take out the people in thousands you will find ground-rents rise at once and the whole state of matters practically repeated in the country. The *Land* is the key!'[37]

Although there was a correlation between the availability of cheap railway transport and the development of working class suburbs – as the case of the GER's services to north east London illustrated – this disguised the importance of housing costs. There was a limit to the rent affordable by working-class families – between £25–£35 per annum – beyond which the cost of travel was an irrelevance. Thus in London, as Dr Kellett's study has shown, this limited the choice of new suburban residence to districts such as Walthamstow and Edmonton or, for the slightly better off, West Kensington and Queen's Park. Even with cheap fares a suburb like Wimbledon and a host of others at similar distances from central London, were inaccessible to the working class because there was simply not the housing at the right price.[38] The crucial condition, as the Royal Commission on the Housing of the Working Classes had recognised in 1884, was that 'the fares must not exceed the difference between the rent of their homes in the overcrowded districts which ought to be relieved and the lower rents in the suburbs.'[39]

But this is not to absolve the railway companies completely. Many did have objections to extending the scope and extent of workmen's services. The handling of expanding suburban traffic was becoming an increasingly difficult task for operational reasons. The deployment of engines, rolling stock and staff had to be crammed into two relatively short morning and evening peaks, leaving a considerable proportion of resources unproductive for the rest of the day. Moreover, suburban trains occupied valuable line capacity on the restricted approaches to terminal stations. Expensive alterations to stations and track were often necessary to accommodate suburban traffic. The GNR, to cite one company's experience, was forced to duplicate the main line over the eight miles from Wood Green to Potter's Bar, double five of its tunnels and treble the Copenhagen and Maiden tunnels.[40]

The mixing of passengers of different social classes also raised objections. Some railway managers claimed that the habits, language and clothing of working men could be offensive to other passengers. Even William Birt, the general manager of the GER, felt uneasy about the social graces of the passengers attracted by his company's generous provision of workmen's services. 'I should be very sorry indeed', he admitted, 'to allow any respectable female connected with my household to travel third class upon the Great Eastern Railway during those hours of the day in which the workers are travelling.'[41] The major 'difficulties' occurred in the evening peak when 'well-to-do City men and their wives and daughters' might have to vie with working men for platform space. It was also complained that working-class passengers constantly evaded payment of fares and damaged property. 'We have so many mischievous people', the manager of the Metropolitan Railway observed, 'that we are obliged to remove all straps from the third-class carriages; we have carriages continually cut.'[42] Conversely, ensuring that only 'artisans, mechanics and daily labourers' and not clerks and shop workers made use of cheap travel facilities also exercised the minds of railway managements, often to little avail.

But the resistance to workmen's trains was often based on hard-headed commercial considerations rather than class snobbery. As Dr Kellett's authoritative study has shown, the companies frequently received little financial reward when a district developed into railway suburb. Communities closest to the cities, those likely to prove most attractive to working-class families, usually depended on road rather than rail services for their essential supplies of food, coal and other commodities. At the same time the transformation of a locality into burgeoning suburb often resulted in the railway, already perhaps paying a disproportionate share of local rates, having to shoulder an even heavier burden. Nor could they offset this against the profits to be made from rising land values since as operating railway companies they were prevented from speculating in the land market.[43] This left the companies with the extra revenue from the passengers to the new suburbs. But how valuable was this, especially where the community was primarily a working-class one and many of the commuters travelled at concessionary fares?

It was generally assumed that such services were uneconomic to operate. Subscribing to this view the Royal Commission on the Housing of the Working Classes believed that the 'state has interfered in this matter in the public interest, rather with reference to what the working classes can afford than to what will pay the companies.'[44] Even the GER was circumspect about the value of its cheap suburban traffic. As the railway writer W. M. Acworth explained: 'Ask a Great Eastern official if these low rates pay? "Well, no, perhaps. Directly they only just pay their working expenses, but indirectly they pay us. The workmen's wives and families, and the tradesmen who serve them, travel up and down the line at ordinary fares. . . . You can't settle a great population down in a place without finding employment for the railway that serves it".'[45] Other companies were unequivocal: both the Metropolitan and LBSC claimed that cheap fare passengers were carried at a direct loss. Companies like the GWR, LNWR and Midland preferred to concentrate on main line traffic. Since none of these companies served really extensive working-class districts, they were unlikely to be persuaded into a radical extension of cheap fare services which besides offering little clear commercial advantage would have jeopardised existing traffic arrangements.

Nevertheless, by the time of the First World War the cheap fare had been 'clearly recognised' as a critical factor in determining the distribution of the population, particularly in the Metropolis.[46] On the south side of London about twenty five per cent of all suburban railway passengers were, by 1912, buying workmen's tickets and within a zone extending six to eight miles from central London about forty per cent of all commuters were travelling on workmen's tickets.[47] The twopenny ticket was the yardstick by which cheap travel provision was measured, since it was considered as being 'within reach of the largest body of workpeople.' In 1905 the range of travel possible on such tickets was 21 miles in east London, 12 miles in west London, 11 miles in north London and 8 miles in south London. By 1913 the range had been extended beyond the County boundary on some lines.[48]

Still, cheap fare passengers comprised a relatively small proportion of London's daily suburban rail traffic. In the early 1900s those travelling on twopenny tickets amounted to only seven per cent of the total.[49] When one takes into account the uneven distribution of workmen's fares around London and the extensive provision for cheap fare traffic made by the electric tramways, the railway's contribution to the daily transit needs of the working class is placed in perspective. The railway suburbs, the passengers they spawned and the platform etiquette of their stations remained overwhelmingly middle class. Moreover, the housing problems which had inspired the provision of cheap fares had not been solved by 1914. Although cheap fares provided opportunities for better paid workers to move to the suburbs here too they might still find extensive areas of 'unplanned, unpleasant, and often insanitary' housing.[50]

Railways and Suburban Passengers Between the Wars

The drift of the population from city centres to the suburbs became the 'most prominent feature' in the distribution of population after the First World War and contributed to a doubling of the built-up area of the country from six to ten per cent between the Wars.[51] Of the 4.3 million houses built in Britain between the Wars about two thirds were private. Many of these were small detached and semi-detached houses built on green field estates that extended the limits of suburbia outwards in an uncontrolled sprawl. The remaining third – nearly 1.5 million houses – were built by local authorities. A start on council house building had been made in several cities before 1914, but housing needs had outstripped local authority resources. After the war the availability of government subsidies enabled the municipalities to make a more determined attack on housing problems and the period witnessed the building of the first large scale council estates, such as the London County Council's Becontree estate in Essex and Manchester Corporation's Wythenshawe estate to the south of Manchester.

Many of the inter-war suburbs became more than just dormitories. With their own employment opportunities, shopping, educational and entertainment facilities, they were to some extent self-supporting. Nevertheless, with large numbers of people still needing to travel to work in town, the provision of adequate transport links was essential. The railway continued to fulfil an important, often vital, role in this respect. But its position was increasingly under challenge from new competitors – the motor bus and private car. As we have seen, in communities closer to the inner cities the electric tramway had already become a far more significant carrier of suburban passengers than the railway. From the 1920s both railway and tramway began to suffer from the proliferation of competitive bus services. In many of the new housing estates, private and council alike, it was the more flexible services of the bus which provided the principal means of getting to work, school and the shops.

Although proximity to a railway station was frequently used by developers as a selling point for their new suburban homes, for an increasing number of residents the station was no longer within walking distance. Often the bus provided the first stage in the journey to work, acting as feeder from some far-flung part of the estate to the station. Council estates too often suffered from this problem. This was the case at Becontree which, although skirted by railways, was for a long time devoid of convenient stations. Until the rebuilding of Gale Street Halt at Becontree and the opening of several other new stations in the early 1930s, many Becontree residents whose work remained in London found it necessary to take a bus to Ilford where connections with trains to town could be made.[52]

The impact of the rise of motor transport on the suburban railway is difficult to ascertain with any precision. Since road transport services were more flexible than either the railway or tramway it allowed new traffic flows to develop. It is reasonable to assume, therefore, that road transport generated new traffic where the railway was not even in a position to compete. But there is little doubt that the suburban railway suffered at the hands of road transport. One estimate suggests that between 250–300 million passenger journeys were lost to road transport by 1937, a large proportion of which was on the short or medium distance services

Houses for all.

THE abnormal development of the immediate suburbs of London has caused them to become a part of the Metropolis, separate from it by name alone, and it is for this reason that those who seek quiet, combined with a healthy and restorative atmosphere, must go farther afield, away from the din and bustle of the city, the scene of their daily labours.

The residential districts served by the Metropolitan Railway lie in the north-west of Middlesex, the south-west of Hertfordshire, and in the heart of historic Bucks and the fertile Vale of Aylesbury, extending to the ancient town of that name.

Situate throughout on high ground, amid pastural and woodland scenery, these varied localities possess distinctive advantages. Foremost amongst them being their bracing health-giving properties, their accessibility from Town, rendered possible by the Company's unrivalled train service, the low Season Ticket rates, to suit the most slender purse, the splendid Golf Links that are to be found at hand in all the districts, and the efficient shopping and educational facilities obtaining throughout.

Outstanding among the Building Estates in Metro-land are those owned by the Metropolitan Railway Country Estates, Ltd., and with their vigorous programme of development, house-seeker and investor alike would be well advised to consider the sterling qualities of these unique Estates.

The Commercial Manager, Metropolitan Railway, Baker St. Station, will gladly furnish fullest information relating to the above Estates and cordially invites use of the non-committal coupon below.

COMMERCIAL MANAGER,
METROPOLITAN RAILWAY,
BAKER ST. STATION, N.W.1.

Please send fullest information of Houses and Land available in Metro-land.

NAME...

ADDRESS ....

....

Few railway companies did more to promote life in suburbia than the Metropolitan (courtesy of the London Transport Museum).

where buses offered convenient and cheap services.[53]

But the picture was not entirely bleak for the suburban railway. In London, where suburban traffic was the most extensive, the railway companies fought back with station improvements and suburban extensions. In some cases developers subsidised the opening of new stations, while many older stations, particularly on the Underground and Southern Railway, were modernised and extended to accommodate growing passenger traffic. In addition there were several new building projects during this period, notably extensions of the City & South London and Piccadilly lines into the suburbs at Hendon, Edgware, Hounslow West, Cockfosters and Uxbridge.[54]

Apart from the Southern Railway, one of the most progressive suburban railways during this period was the Metropolitan. Through a subsidiary company, the Metropolitan Railway Country Estates Ltd, the Metropolitan was actively involved in the purchase and development of suburban estates close to its lines. By the early 1920s it had commenced building at three locations – Kingsbury ajoining Neasden station, the Chalk Hill estate at Wembley, and the Cedars estate between Rickmansworth and Chorley Wood. 'The object in selecting these estates', admitted an unabashed general manager of the Metropolitan, 'was to enable them to serve different classes of residents. The houses at Kingsbury are of the small villa type; those at Chalk Hill are of a somewhat larger class with more ground allotted to them, and the whole of the Cedars estate is being devoted to detached houses of a more pretentious type with a minimum of one acre of land.'[55] To accommodate the growing traffic from these and other estates in Middlesex, Hertfordshire and Buckinghamshire – Metroland as the posters proclaimed – the Company was forced to increase the capacity of its lines and stations in the London area. It also proceeded with electrification to Rickmansworth, while for the more affluent commuters of Aylesbury and Chesham the resplendent comfort of golf and tennis club was replicated in its service of Pullman cars on certain trains.

Suburban services on the surface lines of the main line companies also underwent change and improvement during these years. The Southern Railway with perhaps the most complex inheritance from pre-grouping days nonetheless actively developed its suburban services. Under the influence of Herbert Walker the company pressed ahead with an ambitious programme of electrification, the foundations of which had been laid in the pre-war period. Electric trains began running to Coulsden North and Sutton on the former LBSC lines in 1925. In the same year work was begun on electrifying the lines formerly owned by the LSWR and South Eastern and Chatham. By 1926 electric trains were running out of Victoria, Charing Cross and Cannon Street to Crystal Palace, Beckenham, Elmers End, Addiscombe and along the North Kent and Dartford lines.[56] The effects were often startling. Whereas some of the company's steam hauled suburban services had been losing traffic, electric services could reverse the trend. By 1928 total passenger journeys on the Southern electrified lines had increased by six million over the previous year; by 1930 the company's shareholders were told that 'the increase in traffic in the electrified area is progressing at a pace which has exceeded all expectations.'[57] By this time a start had been made on electrifying the remaining London suburban lines of the former Brighton company and in 1932 a start was made on extending the live rail down the main line to the south coast.

Developments on the suburban lines owned by the LMS, LNER and GWR were less innovative. Apart from the electrification of the former LNWR line from Euston/Broad Street to Watford there was no counterpart to the Southern's efforts. Suburban services remained steam hauled and in many cases the pre-war pattern of services maintained. The major exception was the GER lines out of Liverpool Street. Prior to the Grouping the company had intensified its service of steam trains. The 'Jazz' service, as it was known, which commenced in 1920 was essentially a cut price alternative to electrification. After grouping the LNER considered electrification out of Liverpool Street and also on the former Great Northern lines out of King's Cross, but the projected costs dissuaded the company from modernising its suburban services and they remained for many passengers a perennial source of complaint.[58] The only LNER electrification project actually commenced during this period was on the former GER line to Shenfield. However, this was part of a wider initiative involving government investment and the newly created London Passenger Transport Board (1933) which had assumed responsibility for all major capital projects affecting London's suburban railways. Hopes that the government might look favourably on electrification of the Great Northern lines went unfulfilled, the LPTB giving priority to extensions to the tube system.

By the Second World War London's suburban system was by far the most extensive and complex in Britain. Parts of it were already antiquated, but a substantial portion had been modernised with electric trains, new signalling, stations and extensions. A start had also been made with the creation of the LPTB on the daunting task of coordinating transport services in the capital. Electrification was clearly the major key to improving suburban services as the success of the Southern's efforts had demonstrated. This was echoed by the Royal Commission on Transport in 1930 which concluded 'that it would be greatly to the interests of the railway companies, and at the same time tend to the great convenience of the public, if all suburban services were electrified, not merely in the London area but in every district where there is intensive suburban passenger traffic.'[59]

But such hopes were not to be realised. Of the 990 route miles electrified in Britain by 1939, the Southern's lines together with those controlled by the LPTB accounted for no less than 800.[60] The bulk of the remaining electrified lines were to be found on Merseyside and Tyneside – lines which had been converted by their pre-grouping owners. Apart from some additional electrification around Manchester there was no positive response to the recommendations of the Royal Commission. The failure to innovate further, while it cannot be laid solely at the door of the companies, without doubt left the suburban railways increasingly exposed to competition from road transport services especially in the modern era of mass motoring. It was not until after the creation of the various regional passenger transport authorities in the late 1960s that more strenuous efforts were made in some areas to improve and modernise the services provided by suburban railways.

6
Railway Journeys for Leisure

Hundreds of thousands of dwellers in "populous cities pent," would but for the railways have been compelled to pass the holidays amid the familiar squalor of their everyday life. ... Our great manufacturing cities pour forth their tide of human life into the neighbouring hills and moorlands and seaside places of resort.

Railway News, 1889

Railway travel, epitomised by the excursion train at cheap fares, was in itself a new form of leisure activity, providing opportunities to sample the pleasures of the cities, to spend a day at the seaside or in the country, or to attend a variety of sporting and social events. Few of these activities, of course, were new to the railway age; but the railway's carrying capacity combined with its speed, relatively low fares and wide choice of destinations ensured that railway journeys for leisure purposes gradually became accessible to all but the poorest or most remote sections of Victorian society. While not all travel for leisure was confined to excursion trains or even the railway, in the first section of this chapter we shall focus on the development of the excursion train and its role in the transformation of a wide variety of leisure pursuits. In the second section attention is switched to the relationship between the railway, the growth of the resorts and the holidaymaker. The response of the railways to the growing popularity of leisure travel, the operational implications of providing extra (or special) trains for the needs of excursionists and their attempts to publicise railway travel services and facilities are considered more fully in subsequent chapters.

The Development of the Excursion Train

The railway journey for leisure needs to be viewed in the context of wider changes in the economy and society traditionally associated with the 'Industrial Revolution'. In recent years historians have

THE ATTRACTIONS
OF
MERRIE MORECAMBE
ARE
IRRESISTIBLE

Beautiful Bay
Golden Sands
Ample Accommodation
Convenient Centre
FOR
English Lakes

TRAVEL FROM
THE CENTRAL STATION

Tourist Tickets Daily   Cheap Excursions Weekly

EXCURSION FARES	4 DAY 10/	8 DAY 17/	16 DAY 18/

BOOKLET FREE AT THE ENQUIRY OFFICE

A handpainted bill on Central Station, Glasgow, in the Summer of 1913 (by courtesy of the Tourism and Attractions Department, Sefton MBC).

begun to question the suddenness of change implied by this term. In place of the conventional emphasis on discontinuity, new technology and the factory, the picture of industrialisation is presented as one of transition and long-run development, of restricted and localised change, of the survival of handicraft industries, traditional technologies and small workshops.[1] But if the 'triumph' of the factory was neither as extensive nor as rapid as sometimes portrayed, if by mid century a majority of the labour force still worked in agriculture, domestic service or trades yet to be transformed in technique and organisation, in the longer term the emergence of an industrial economy coupled with class-based urban living brought major changes to the way society worked and played. Industrialisation involved not just a restructuring of work habits and discipline, but arguably an 'onslaught' on traditional forms of recreations and pastimes.[2]

Railway travel was to play an important part in these changes: it allowed both the adaptation of older leisure activities and customs to the exigencies of a new urban-industrial order and enabled alternative forms of 'rational' enjoyment to develop. The changing character of popular holiday festivities such as the Lancashire wakes illustrates this process. Originally religious festivals, by the late eighteenth century the wakes in Lancashire had become predominantly secular events – celebrations of community identity with the emphasis partly on commercial attractions such as the public house and fairground, yet retaining a tradition of 'home based hospitality and conviviality'.[3] But as the factory economy of Lancashire advanced, so the wakes were increasingly subject to a range of pressures which began to undermine and eventually transform their character. The pernicious effects of the trade cycle might periodically strain the ability to enjoy the convivial aspects of the wakes. House building and other urban development undoubtedly encroached upon those areas traditionally given over to wakes activities. At the same time there were those in authority who began to view the wakes as a potential threat to property and public order, occasions which ought to be discouraged or their appeal minimised by encouraging people to look to alternative 'rational recreations' for their enjoyment.[4]

The railway excursion could serve as just such an alternative. Day trips by train to the seaside during the period traditionally given over to the wakes were apparently established by the 1840s. At this stage there was no question of excursions killing off the wakes celebrations – on the contrary, by arriving back in the late afternoon it was possible to have a day by the sea and still indulge in the local festivities during the evening. But from the 1870s, when longer stays at the seaside were becoming increasingly popular amongst Lancashire's factory operatives, the railway excursion and the rival attractions of the seaside began to undermine the old-style wakes. The railway excursion did not destroy the wakes; rather it helped to modify them and preserve their importance in a new guise to the factory towns of the region.

Here, then, was one approach to the growing 'problem' of the leisure of the masses. If the industrial worker had to be left with some free time – and for those in full-time industrial employment there might be precious little of that – then it should not be whiled away in traditional pursuits which some perceived as conducive to idleness, vice or potentially riotous gatherings. The railway excursion seemed to offer an important counter attraction. 'The advantages of these railway excursions are many', the *Manchester Guardian* declared in 1845, 'but amongst their principal social benefits . . . we may notice that they are greatly conducive to health, by combining pure air with the active exercise of field sports, that they are not less productive of cheerful, sober, and innocent enjoyment.' That they were also 'eminently social and domestic in their character' was considered a strong point in their favour, particularly when compared to the traditional Whitsuntide race meetings on Kersal Moor which, it was lamented, regularly produced 'tumultuous, disorderly, and intemperate scenes . . . in which wives and children cannot and ought not to participate.'[5]

The promotion of a 'rational' form of entertainment enjoyable by the whole family seemed to justify the railway excursion. That they could also be free of the intemperance often associated with traditional leisure activities also caught the attention of some observers. 'Excursion trains', noted *Herapath's Railway Journal* in 1850, 'have a very sensible effect on diminishing the consumption of wine and spirits . . . and . . . the publicans and theatres complain loudly against them. . . . Here is a good plainly and positively produced by excursion trains, the diminution of intemperance.'[6]

To claim, as Herapath went on to do, that excursion trains were effecting 'a great moral revolution' was perhaps an exaggeration, but there is no doubting the link between the railway and the cause of temperance. Had not Thomas Cook, populariser if not the originator of the railway excursion at cheap fares, organised his famous first excursion of 1841 in the cause of temperance? 'About midway between Harborough and Leicester', Cook later recalled, 'a thought flashed through my brain, what a glorious thing it would be if the newly-developed powers of railways and locomotion could be made subservient to the promotion of temperance!'[7] Cook began organising his purely commercial excursions in 1845, but the impetus provided by the temperance movement – sufficient to fill 25 'tubs' with some 500 people each paying a shilling for the eleven mile journey between Leicester and Loughborough in 1841 – should not be neglected. Certainly the temperance excursion became a fairly common occurrence in mid-Victorian years and frequently brought large numbers of passengers to the railways. A Grand Temperance demonstration at Swarthmore in July 1857, for example, attracted some 6,000 people, many of them travelling on 'monster' excursion trains from Manchester and Preston and 'heavy' trains from the towns of Lancaster, Kendal and Whitehaven.[8]

In other ways too, the railway excursion could be perceived as a civilising influence. Their benefits, particularly their ability to transport large numbers of workers to places of 'healthful recreation', soon attracted the attention of employers. Excursions organised by employers might serve a variety of purposes, from a simple desire to promote good will and loyalty to the firm, to a paternalistic and perhaps moralistic drive 'to offer opportunities for "rational enjoyment", remoulding the pattern of popular recreations in a desired image.'[9] The latter might be reflected clearly in the determination to organise the excursionists' day for them. For instance, when Mr Slater, a biscuit manufacturer from Carlisle, and his employees visited the Lake District in 1854, their agenda was such to invite comment from the *Westmorland Gazette*: 'On arrival at Bowness, Mr Slater and his companions took the steamer to Ambleside visiting Stockgill Force, the beautiful new church, Rydal Mount, Harriet Martineau's and other places of note and interest.'

Such aesthetic and spiritual considerations were perhaps not typical of excursion programmes even where the employer was footing the bill. Nevertheless, it was significant that as early as 1845 the Factory Inspectors had not only advised employers of the ease with which carriages could be hired for summer excursions, but had also highlighted one case where tickets could only be acquired on proof of good conduct, 'as evidenced by attendance at some place of instruction or of public worship.'[10] Certainly the mid-Victorian period saw the heyday of company-sponsored excursions, many of them originating in the manufacturing districts of Lancashire, the West Riding and the Midlands.

In the later Victorian period the excursions organised by small- and medium-sized employers were overshadowed by those sponsored by large-scale companies. Amongst the most spectacular were those organised by the brewers Bass, Ratcliffe and Gretton of Burton. The annual Bass outings were mammoth railway occasions regularly involving some 10,000 employees and guests. Although the company could hardly claim temperance as the inspiration for their trips, the emphasis was nonetheless on orderly behaviour and sobriety. Brochures issued to each employee implored 'all persons to be quiet and orderly on the journeys, on the steamers, at the various Places of Amusement, in the Streets and generally throughout the day.' On the journey itself the non-segregation of foremen and men presumably allowed for some carryover of workplace discipline beyond the factory gate. On the trip to Great Yarmouth in 1893, to cite one case, 11 of the 15 trains were given over to the foremen, men, wives and families of the brewery itself, the remaining 4 being given over to clerks, customers, estate workers and friends. Travel arrangements were to be adhered to strictly, the brochure making it clear that anyone breaking 'this urgent regulation will be LEFT BEHIND at Burton or Great Yarmouth.'[11]

As major shareholders and customers of the Midland Railway, the Bass family was more favourably placed than most to undertake such exceptionally large excursions – over 200 carriages, complicated engine movements and sole possession of long stretches of main lines, stations and sidings were normally required. But despite the differences in scale, Bass and other employers shared with groups as disparate as temperance and friendly societies, Sunday Schools, Mechanics' Institutes and trade unions an interest in promoting the railway excursion as an important counter-attraction to less desirable popular recreations. Industrial paternalism, self-improvement, evangelism or philanthropy: each might be equally well-served by the organisation of an excursion train and the imposition of a 'suitable' programme of events.

Arguably excursions of this description came of age during the period of the Great Exhibition in 1851. This self-conscious celebration of Britain's commercial and industrial success was a major public attraction and provided the railways with a unique opportunity to demonstrate their importance to such events. Representatives of the railway companies, under some pressure from the exhibition organisers, had agreed to provide cheap travel facilities. By the end of the Exhibition some six million visitors had attended, many of them arriving by excursion train. The fact that such huge crowds – including both agricultural labourers and northern factory workers – could assemble in the capital city without presenting any serious threat to public order, impressed many contemporaries and arguably underlined the social acceptability of the excursionist.[12]

Yet this argument cannot be accepted without reservation. Not all excursions were of the type organised by church, chapel or employers and not all excursionists were drawn from the ranks of 'respectable' artisans. Far from being a civilising influence the railway excursion might offend a variety of Victorian sensibilities and provoke considerable opposition as a consequence. The Lord's Day Observance Society, for example, was a persistent, if unsuccessful, critic of the attempts by the railway companies to fill their excess capacity on Sundays with excursion trains. On such occasions, it was complained, 'God's Day is dishonoured and God's creations crushed that the directors may present a flattering report to their shareholders and pay the ½ per cent more dividend.'[13]

Moral tracts, too, warned of the pitfalls awaiting those who succumbed to the temptations of a Sunday excursion. The experience of Harry Lyte, a ficticious workman from Whitechapel, served as an example to others. Having ignored the advice of a workmate to 'let the Sunday excursions alone' he allowed himself and his family to be lured on a trip to Brighton. The day was a litany of misfortunes: a fretful baby, one child with a cut hand, a domestic row after Harry had returned from the ale-house 'flushed and merry', and a child lost in the crowded station as the train was about to depart. 'The trip hasn't done us much good', admitted poor Harry on his return, 'we've had nothing for the mind . . . we've had a good many discomforts, and we're as tired as dogs.' It was left to his workmate to make the inevitable admission for him: 'Wheel round the question as you will, and make what excuses you will for these Sunday excursions, they are sinful.'[14]

While Sunday excursions incurred the wrath of the Sabbatarians, the willingness of the railway companies to meet the demand for excursions on other days might raise different problems. Monday excursions in particular clashed with the desire of many employers to impose on their workers more regular work habits and a greater sense of time discipline. This was evident in Birmingham where skilled workers on piece rates maintained, until well into the nineteenth century, the tradition of Saint Monday, devoting Sunday and Monday (Tuesday too if earnings were sufficient) to relaxation, catching up on their work towards the end of the week. Accordingly the earliest excursions out of Birmingham – the first ran in 1841 – tended to depart on Mondays rather than Sundays, or the Saturdays advocated by Sabbatarians and the Early Closing Association. In 1846 only six of twenty two Birmingham excursions did not depart on a Monday.[15] Nor it seems was the market for Monday excursions confined to the workshop dominated economy of Birmingham. As late as 1850 *Herapath's Railway Journal* was calling for the provision of cheap excursions for London trippers on Mondays and even Tuesdays 'for our pleasure seeking Londoners, do frequently enlarge their Saint's Calender, and add Saint Tuesday to Saint Monday.'[16]

But on whatever day the excursionists travelled, their arrival *en masse* at the growing number of watering and pleasure resorts around the coastline of Britain was not always greeted with enthusiasm. According to one historian of the British seaside resort, they provided something of a culture shock to the residents and visitors of some of the more genteel and pretentious resorts. Their tastes in amusements, their noise and disregard for local byelaws, their heavy drinking and even their appearance, it is suggested, led many to view the day tripper with distaste.[17] But the real fear was that the availability of cheap excursions might swamp such resorts with working-class trippers and deter better-class visitors in the future. The self-styled 'Aristocratic Saltburn', for instance, was one of several resorts which at various times petitioned the local railway company to stop running excursions from nearby industrial towns.[18]

Concern for the moral turpitude of the nation combined with more traditional fears for public order also served to bring the railway excursion into disrepute. Such was the case when the railway companies pandered to the public's appetite for 'sensation' and carried excursionists to public executions. Excursion trains were advertised to several executions in mid-Victorian years, among them the hanging of a multiple murderer at Liverpool gaol in 1848 when an estimated 100,000 spectators gathered for the event. Marginally less offensive, though increasingly interpreted as an affront to the conscience of mid-Victorian liberalism, was the role of the excursion train in taking large crowds to prize-fights. The SER and LCDR were remarkably dogged servants of the prize-fight promoters. As the authorities in London became less tolerant of prize fighting these companies obliged the organisers by taking large numbers of spectators – up to 2,000 to one fight in 1859 – to 'quieter' locations out of town.[19] It was no coincidence that the reform of boxing included attempts, eventually realised in 1868, to forbid the railways from running excursions to prize-fights.[20]

As other sports developed into national spectator events they raised a variety of public order and crowd control problems. Again there was nothing new about rowdy elements accompanying sporting occasions. But cheap and rapid travel by excursions (supplemented by regular services) made the problems more widespread. Horse racing in particular benefitted from the running of excursion trains: by drawing spectators from a wide hinterland local races could be either turned into national events or, at the very least, rescued from oblivion. But the assembly of large crowds at such events was not unattended by 'social evils'. As early as 1838 a mob of excursionists bound for Epsom racecourse, one of many that ringed London, began to riot at the Nine Elms terminus of the LSWR when it became clear that there were not enough trains to carry them.[21] In Brighton it was claimed that serious crimes committed by outsiders, particularly from London, increased 'at the time of the races when criminals of all classes flock to the town.'[22] Such problems were not confined to racing – most of the major spectator events attracted similar anti-social elements and presented analogous threats to public order.

Railway excursions with these associations were a very different proposition to those with social and moral improvement as their keynote. To some extent the differences may be explained by the distinction between the formal or private excursions organised by employers, churches, societies and clubs, and the informal excursions open to the general public and organised on a purely commercial basis. The former, it has been argued, were often community occasions subject to the approbation of bosses, family or neighbours and their participants more respectable and less likely to misbehave. According to this line of argument the absence of such sanctions on informal trips might explain their tendency towards 'anti-social accompaniments.'[23]

However, it is clear that excursions of the formal variety were not immune from anti-social behaviour – drunkenness on temperance outings was not unknown, while excursionists on day trips organised by employers were sometimes involved in 'horse-play' or worse, as a riot at Southend in 1874 confirms.[24] The excursion business was in any case increasingly dominated by the informal or commercial trips as the railway companies and other 'factors' began to realise the extent of the demand for such travel and devoted more of their energies to attracting a greater share of traffic. The development of excursions into a popular recreation owed more to this than any deliberate attempts to use the railway as an agent of social control.[25] Although excursions could and did assist those who sought to impose on workers their own ideas of what constituted a civilised or respectable use of leisure time, for the most part the business was underpinned by a commercial relationship between railway and passenger. As the next section will seek to demonstrate the same was true of the wider relationship between the railways, the holidaymaker and the holiday resorts.

Railways, Resorts and the Holidaymaker

On the eve of the railway age the market for personal travel, especially for leisure purposes, was already expanding. Road and water transport catered for this market sufficiently well to allow the development of a growing number of spa and resort towns – places

THE POPULAR
BRITISH SUMMER
RESORTS

ISLE OF MAN
NORTH OF IRELAND
SCOTLAND
LANCASHIRE COAST
PEAK DISTRICT
YORKSHIRE MOORS
LAKE DISTRICT

are conveniently reached by the Midland Railway

To any of these districts you can make
the journey a pleasant part of your
holiday if you travel by the Midland

An advertisement for the holiday resorts and regions served by the Midland
Railway: one of many which appeared in the growing number of 'holiday' booklets
published before the Grouping.

visited for health and/or social reasons by those with sufficient resources and time to devote to serious leisure. Coaching services to these centres multiplied considerably during the late eighteenth and early nineteenth centuries, while coastal shipping services also provided visitors to some resorts with a more convenient and cheaper alternative. Already by 1792, for example, some 18,000 people were transported by 'well appointed hoys' from London to various Kentish coastal resorts.[26] Steamboat services introduced on the major river estuaries after 1815 did much to stimulate traffic to nearby resort towns, their cheaper fares and novelty widening the appeal of travel for leisure purposes. The majority of such travellers were drawn predominantly from the middle ranks of society, but the appeal of the sea and resorts extended much further than this: already by the early nineteenth century watering places along the Lancashire coast were visited by significant numbers of urban workers, many of them travelling by cart or on foot.

The railway had the effect of extending still further the market for travel to seaside and inland watering places. The relatively cheap and, by previous standards, rapid transport it made possible was to be a vital factor in the development of the seaside holiday into a popular institution. However, this did not happen overnight. Initally it was middle-class families who benefitted most – those with sufficient income and time to emulate the leisure habits of their social superiors and spend a week, perhaps longer, at the seaside. By the 1860s seaside resorts and holidays away from home were still predominantly the preserve of the middle-class. For working-class families access to the resorts remained limited to day trips by excursion train. It was not until the last quarter of the century that industrial workers in some districts began to enjoy a sufficient level of family income and officially recognised (if unpaid) annual holidays to begin contemplating taking a short break away from home.[27]

It was not, therefore, until relatively late in the nineteenth century that the mass holiday-making industry began to emerge and with it the really big resorts such as Blackpool, Brighton, Scarborough, Weston-super-Mare and several others catering for a mass, mainly lower middle- and working-class, market. The smaller and more select resorts attractive to a largely middle-class clientele remained, but it was the big resorts attracting millions of visitors annually that dominated the holiday industry and cemented the role of the railway in the mass travel market, a role it retained until challenged and eventually supplanted by other forms of transport serving rather different holiday tastes during the second half of the twentieth century.

Without the railways the Victorian resorts could not have developed as they did. Yet the extent of the railway's contribution to their growth should not be exaggerated. It was rare for the railway to create an entirely new resort. There were some, along the North Wales coast for instance, that hardly existed until the coming of the railway. But in the main the railway had the effect of allowing established resorts such as Brighton and Scarborough to achieve further growth potential, or of allowing small bathing villages, such as Blackpool and Southport, to emerge as genuine resort towns catering for masses of holidaymakers. For all that, the railway companies themselves often had little direct role in the expansion of the resort towns.

The motives behind the building of railway lines to the sea are revealing. The Fylde coast was opened up originally by a railway built to serve the new port of Fleetwood, the lines to Blackpool and St Annes mere 'branch' lines, their importance apparent only later; the North Wales coast was made accessible by a 'main' line to Holyhead built primarily to carry Irish traffic to and from Holyhead; the Cumbrian and Cleveland coasts were opened up to railways by the lure of mineral traffic; the North Cornwall coast at Newquay by the possibilities of exporting china clay. Even established resorts, Brighton serves as the premier example, offered promoters the prospect of established and growing residential traffic – far more important on a year-round basis than highly seasonal and competitive holiday traffic.

Some resorts, it is true, received considerable attention from the railway companies that served them. In Cleethorpes, Skegness and Silloth, to cite some well-chronicled cases, railway investment in land, property and other facilities was designed to aid development into holiday resort and stimulate new passenger traffic.[28] But overall, as John Walton's studies have revealed, the railway's role in resort development was largely a passive one.[29] This was certainly the experience of the major growth resorts of south Lancashire. Holiday interests in these resorts complained of the poor services offered by the railway companies, especially the LYR. Although this company redeemed itself slightly through its extensive provision of excursion facilities, significantly the company cut back on such services during the early 1870s at precisely the time when demand for holidays away from home was beginning to manifest itself amongst the region's working class.

Demand, as Dr Walton argues, was the key factor. The mass holiday-making industry developed earliest and furthest in industrial Lancashire and the West Riding because of cultural and economic factors affecting the way in which working families chose to spend their leisure time. The relatively high level and regularity of family incomes; a tradition of belonging to savings clubs which might easily be turned to the needs of an annual holiday; the emergence of the wakes weeks as officially recognised annual holiday periods when factories, whole towns almost, closed down: these factors promoted a demand for working-class holidays by the sea in advance of workers in other industrial districts.[30]

Contrast the experience of Teeside in North East England. A large working-class population working in iron and steel, shipbuilding and other heavy industries might have been expected to develop a similar taste for the seaside holiday. But serious trade depressions, severe fluctuations in earnings and a consequent inability to save on a regular basis, an absence of opportunities for working class wives and children to contribute to family incomes, and a reluctance by employers to sanction an annual holiday period restricted the growth of demand on the pattern of the North West. Instead, as one study of resort development around the mouth of the Tees has observed: 'Any surpluses were usually spent on drink, gambling, or removal to better accommodation, rather than on seaside trips.'[31]

Beyond the obvious effect of channeling large numbers into those resorts with rail connections, the railway also played only a relatively minor role in determining where the different social classes chose to spend their holidays. Places like Blackpool, Skegness, Thanet, Southend and others developed as resorts attractive to the lower middle and working classes not simply because of their proximity to large industrial centres, but because they provided accommodation and entertainment suited to the means and tastes of their visitors. In some resorts there were determined efforts to hold back the tide of demand for boarding houses, sideshows and amusements; in others they were openly embraced, the middle and upper classes either 'colonising' more select quarters away from the railway stations and central areas or deserting the resort altogether in favour of more select retreats in the English and Scottish countryside.

Perceptions within the resorts themselves about their role in the holiday market, inter-resort competition and the tastes of visitors were the most important influences over the social tone of resort development. It was a process that sometimes led to conflicts of interest in the resorts themselves. Those who wished to see their resort preserved as a select, largely middle-class, haven of peace and respectability might attempt to restrict the spread of boarding houses, amusements and other attractions. Rearguard actions of this kind were sometimes successful, but in a number of towns might lead to clashes with those who looked forward to greater commercial development.[32] Such clashes were not confined to the seaside resorts. In the English Lake District, for example, the railway created considerable tensions because it threatened to undermine the area's popularity as a playground of the upper-class.

On the eve of railway building the tourist trade of the Lakes was well-established, purists in search of peace and spiritual uplift being joined in increasing numbers by 'distinguished visitors and highly respectable families' from business and the professions. But the arrival of the railway threatened greater disruption from those who Wordsworth contemptuously dismissed as the 'imperfectly educated classes' tempted out of their homes by 'wrestling matches, horse and boat races without number, and pot houses and beer shops.'[33] In short, the railway brought to the surface a latent conflict between those who sought to preserve the Lake District as a retreat for those in search of solitude and those who wished to see the development of the region's tourist potential. Although by the 1870s the district was approachable by rail from all sides, the threat of large numbers of long stay visitors and trippers in search of entertainments and amusements incompatible with the district's scenery and reputation did not materialise on any significant scale.

There was certainly an increase in the number of visitors. A comparison of the pre- and post-railway arrivals in Windermere, always one of the most accessible and popular locations, gives some indication of the scale of change. During 1843–4 nearly 12,000 passengers passed through the Plumgarths toll on the Kendal and Windermere turnpike. After the opening of the Kendal & Windermere Railway in 1847 ten times that number were carried during the first year of operation alone.[34] The railway also made possible day trips to the Lakes. The *Westmorland Gazette* reported in June 1865 that on one Saturday over 1,300 passengers had arrived at Keswick's recently opened station, many of whom were on day trips, while later, in 1883, Whit Monday saw some 10,000 day trippers at Windermere. Yet there were relatively few concessions to commercialism. Trippers tended to be in 'respectable' groups and the tourist trade remained firmly based on a middle- and upper-class clientele staying for a few weeks at a time.

Tourism on this scale reflected the interests of those who wished to preserve the area as an exclusive resort – the resident gentry and large hoteliers with a stake in the established tourist trade. But it also reflected the nature of demand for holidays in regions such as this. Had it been substantially different in character and had the railway companies, especially the powerful LNWR, wished to develop traffic to the Lakes further, then the area's social exclusivity might have been more seriously undermined. There were those – especially traders, small hoteliers and shopkeepers – who stood to gain from a more rapid expansion of the tourist trade. In the late 1870s attempts to quicken up the pace of tourist development were reflected in the merger of the English Lake District Association and the Lake District Advertising Association to form a single body responsible for publicising and promoting the region. But the emphasis remained on attracting the more 'respectable' and affluent visitor. There was no rapid development of accommodation or amusements designed for working-class visitors and despite the railway the tourist centres of the Lake District retained their essentially upper- and middle-class air throughout the nineteenth century.

The Railway Companies and Leisure Travel in the Twentieth Century

By the later nineteenth century the railway companies were becoming increasingly aware of the value of leisure traffic to their

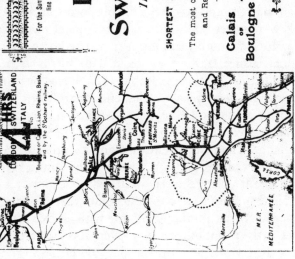

LONDON STATIONS:
Charing Cross, Victoria, Holborn Viaduct, Cannon Street and St. Paul's.

London to Switzerland

NORTHERN AND EASTERN RAILWAYS OF FRANCE

The most comfortable
and Rapid Continental Route

SHORTEST SEA PASSAGE

Of all the routes between England and the Continent, the quickest, the most comfortable and the most popular are those via **Calais or Boulogne, Laon, Rheims to Basle**.

The new steamers "Nord", "Pas-de-Calais", the "Onward", "Douvres", "Calais", "Lord Warden", "Calais-Douvres", "Empress", "Victoria" and "Princess of Wales" belonging to the **Northern of France** and the **South Eastern and Chatham Railway** perform the sea passage to and from **Calais or Boulogne** in 60 to 80 minutes.

These steamers have been specially built to combine speed with comfort and are most luxuriously fitted up.

TRAINS

Throughout the year communication between **Calais or Boulogne and Basle** is assured by two daily express trains, composed of 1st and 2nd class lavatory carriage inter-communicating. The quickest covers, during the summer, the distance of 780 kilom. between **Calais or Boulogne and Basle** in less than 14 hours. The journey between **London and Basle** and vice-versa is performed in 14 h., Lucerne 17 h., Berne 16 h. and Milan in 24 h. only.

During the summer months, the trains of the two Services are provided with through coupés-lits-toilette-carriages between **Boulogne or Calais and Basle**. In the Calais D train there is a sleeping car of the International Sleeping Car Company and dining car between **Boulogne and Laon**. A through dining car is attached to the trains X and Y between **Calais-Basle and Basle-Boulogne**.

LONDON STATIONS:
Charing Cross, Victoria, Holborn Viaduct, Cannon Street and St. Paul's.

South Eastern and Chatham,
AND
Northern and Eastern Railways of France

For the Summer Season 1904, the ALBULA (Engadine) line will be extended to SAINT-MORITZ

London
to
Switzerland
In 14 Hours

SHORTEST SEA PASSAGE (60 Minutes)

The most comfortable
and Rapid Continental Route

Calais
or
Boulogne
-Rheims-Basle

June 1904.

The South Eastern & Chatham and the Northern and Eastern Railways of France combine to promote travel to Switzerland and Italy for the summer season of 1904 (from the R. B. Wilson Collection, Railways Box 5, by permission of the Bodleian Library).

business. In exceptional cases this was reflected in plans to build competing lines to resorts already served by at least one railway. During the 1880s, for instance, Blackpool holiday interests lobbied for better railway facilities and a new line from Manchester to compete with the LYR was mooted. In this case no new railway resulted, but further down the coast at Southport similar agitation did produce a new line: the Southport & Cheshire Lines Extension Railway (opened in 1883), a product of an alliance between the Midland, Great Northern and Manchester, Sheffield & Lincolnshire railways.[35]

More common than competing lines were improvements to station facilities as growing traffic stretched existing accommodation to the limits. For example, the large numbers visiting Scarborough at the turn of the century prompted the building of a special 'excursion' station and the provision of four miles of additional storage sidings. With its two stations and extra locomotive facilities, Scarborough was able to board and despatch ten trains per hour during the peak evening departure period. Facilities at Blackpool were similarly improved and extended at this time, although the combined twenty nine platforms at the resort's two terminals were never really sufficient to cope at peak holiday periods. It was not just holiday traffic which merited such attention. Even occasional leisure traffic was deemed to justify expensive improvements. On the GWR, for example, racegoers were provided with new stations at Newbury and Cheltenham and their trains – especially the 'members and first-class specials' – accorded the privilege of haulage by fast locomotives.

Mass attendance at sporting events demanded extensive railway arrangements. For example, on the occasion of the Grand National the three stations at Aintree were stretched to capacity – 168 ordinary and excursion trains had to be accommodated on race day in 1913.[36] The GNR was another company with an extensive race traffic. By the early twentieth century over 100,000 passengers regularly arrived at Doncaster on the day of the St Leger. The stabling of the 2,500 or so carriages involved required the clearing of locomotives from works sidings and the total suspension of goods traffic. Trains and sidings were numbered and passengers obliged to clamber down onto the track to make their way to the racecourse. All this enabled Doncaster station to remain free of excursion traffic, its normal business continuing with minimal disturbance.[37] The smooth handling of extra traffic on these and other sporting occasions placed great strains on management and staff. By the end of the century LYR railwaymen had to cope with an additional set of operating instructions dealing with seasonal holiday traffic. Running to 150 pages, this gave details of special train workings, track repairs, tickets and even the whistling of engines at certain locations.

The period before the First World War also saw several railway companies consciously attempting to attract more leisure traffic through better services and extensive advertising. Probably the best known of pre-war advertisements was the Great Northern's ageing and rotund figure striding over the legend 'Skegness is so bracing'. This poster campaign was accompanied by the running of cheap half-day excursions which brought large numbers of passengers to the GNR's only major seaside resort—nearly 5,000 people on the last August Bank Holiday before the outbreak of war. More innovative in terms of train services coupled with advertising were the Furness Railway's circular tours of Lakeland some of which combined railway, coastal and coach travel. That the value of advertising was increasingly appreciated is shown in the reactions of a group of shareholders of the Cockermouth, Keswick & Penrith Railway who complained that Keswick was being ignored in promotions of the Lake District – while the virtues of Windermere were extolled all over the Manchester stations, the attractions of Keswick were proclaimed from just one corner of Manchester Exchange.[38]

Of value to the leisure traveller was the introduction of several new long distance train services. The most notable perhaps was the forerunner of the famous 'Cornish Riviera Express' inaugurated by the GWR in the summer of 1904. One of the crack expresses of the period, 'The Limited' as it became known, covered the 264 miles from Paddington to Plymouth in 265 minutes and brought Penzance within seven hours of London. The train was of particular value to the company's holiday traffic (for the first two years it ran in summer only), especially to Cornwall where the holiday industry was growing rapidly. Inter-provincial services also saw some worthwhile improvements. The forerunner of 'The Pines Express' began as a Manchester to Bournemouth restaurant-car train in 1910. Running via the lines of the Somerset & Dorset Railway this was one of several long-distance services later to link the industrial districts of the North with the seaside resorts of the South Coast. In the opposite direction a new service provided by the Midland Railway from 1897 allowed visitors from the South to journey to the Lake District (St Pancras-Lakeside) without a change of train, and provided new competition for the LNWR's through services to Keswick and Windermere.

So far as leisure traffic on the railways was concerned the timing of the outbreak of war in August 1914 could not have been more disruptive. But the anticipated withdrawal and interference with passenger services did not materialise: with a few exceptions most companies had resumed passenger services, including excursions, before the end of the month. Although the wartime Railway Executive Committee imposed a range of restrictions on passenger travel they were neither uniform nor effective. Early in 1915 a number of cheap and excursion fares associated with events such as races, fairs, football matches, and walking and cycling tours were suspended. Yet cheap fares were still available for visits to army camps, whilst 'tourist' tickets and special tickets issued to 'theatrical companies, music hall artistes, choirs, concert and orchestral parties' were also exempted. The restrictions had little effect; many ordinary trains were forced to run in sections so great were the holiday crowds. As Pratt commented in his classic study of the railways during the First World War: 'Having made up their minds to take a holiday they did so, the higher cost of the railway journey notwithstanding. ... Still less would it deter the considerable number of people to whom the war had brought increased earnings or greater profits.'[39]

It was a similar story for the duration of the war – trains duplicated and extra coaches added despite the imposition of more stringent restrictions on cheap and excursion travel. Overall passenger traffic handled by the railways during 1916 exceeded the figure for the last year of peace. This was the prelude to a more determined effort to eradicate 'unnecessary travel' which the authorities believed hampered essential war work. By January 1917 rail services had been severely curtailed and fares increased by up to fifty per cent. Yet in spite of these and other obstacles to travel, plus repeated warning from government of the need to reduce pleasure travel, holiday traffic was again heavy in 1917. The final summer of the war saw the ignomy of one branch of government imploring people not to travel and another issuing thousands of munitions workers vouchers entitling them to travel at cheap rates.

Peace brought no relief to the hard-pressed railway companies. The problems of demobilisation, and the run-down and depleted state of the railways made it difficult to cater for the demand for holiday travel, especially in 1919. The LYR, for instance, faced exceptionally heavy demand for travel to Blackpool and was forced to experiment with a system of regulating travel. Although popularly misconceived as a system of travel rationing, the scheme required passengers to make advance bookings for the peak holiday periods. Under these conditions over one million visitors arrived at Blackpool during the 1919 season.

During the Inter-War years the railway continued to dominate the leisure travel market. For large numbers of working-class families a week, even a weekend, away from home remained beyond their means. For them the railway continued to serve a vital function, providing opportunities for day trips to the sea and other outings. Nevertheless the demand for holiday travel continued to grow during this period. One estimate in 1937 put the total number of people taking a holiday away from home at fifteen million – one in three of the population. Although the number of workers in receipt of holidays with pay gradually increased, the decisive shift in the case of manual workers did not occur until the Holidays With Pay Act of 1938. This lifted the number enjoying annual paid leave from some four million in 1937 to over eleven million in 1939. However, this does not appear to have brought any noticeable increase in the number going away for a holiday – the peak year being 1937. Rising real incomes rather than holidays with pay seem to have been the most important factor in explaining the growth of holidaymaking.[40]

The major Victorian resorts continued to attract large numbers of visitors and the majority travelled to their desired resort by railway train. Blackpool remained the holiday mecca for the masses; it was still attracting seven million visitors a year at the end of the period compared to over five million at Southend, three million at Hastings, two million each at Bournemouth and Southport, and one million at Eastbourne. These popular resorts were served by a range of regular through services supplemented by seasonal extras and excursions. On several lines handling the extra traffic at holiday periods caused major problems for the operating authorities. For example, during the summer season the GWR was forced to run 'The Limited' as four separate trains departing Paddington at five minute intervals. In the same direction the Southern Railway's premier service – the Atlantic Coast Express – was also split; by 1938 eight separate departures were necessary, their running complicated by the inclusion of slip carriages to enable passengers to travel through to various West Country resorts.

Crowded trains and congested tracks were only one aspect of leisure travel in this period. Competition from road transport was growing, as the car and motor bus began to open up new and more flexible opportunities for leisure travel. The threat did not go unnoticed by the railways and the 1930s in particular saw some interesting responses. In 1933 the LNER inaugurated its 'Tourist Trains'. Dedicated to the excursion business, these twelve coach trains in a striking green and cream livery offered to passengers buffet facilities, bucket seating and tables – a far cry from the slow, cramped and uncomfortable trains provided in the early days of excursion travel. The LMS became involved in the provision of holidays. The company, in conjunction with Thomas Cook's, opened a holiday camp at Prestatyn in 1939 in imitation of the successful Butlin's holiday camps, the first of which had opened at Skegness in 1937. By this time all four main line companies had begun to offer holiday-makers the chance to take their holiday literally on rails – in carriages converted into stationary camping coaches parked in a variety of seaside and country locations. These ideas in accommodation were supplemented by more traditional inducements to travel, such as cheap excursion tickets, season tickets (allowing unlimited travel in a particular area) and special facilities for cyclists, walkers and even motorists.

As yet, however, the challenge from the motor vehicle was limited. Although the number of private cars on the roads increased from less than 500,000 in 1924 to over 2 million in 1939, personal motoring remained the preserve of the middle class. But the car, together with the motor coach, did present a serious and long-term threat to the position of the railway as a carrier of leisure traffic. As one analyst of the motor vehicle's impact on society observed:

From the very start it was 'touring' that was seen as the great attraction – the chance to be free and independent of the excursion train, to select one's own destination and to choose one's own route there, to start and return when one pleases undominated by time tables.[41]

The main beneficiaries of such freedom were the smaller coastal resorts and inland villages away from the railway, where the 'discerning' tourist could find peace and beauty. Yet it was worth noting that for some holiday resorts rail-borne holiday traffic probably reached its peak after the Second World War – in the case of the West Country resorts in 1957. With Beeching, mass motoring and motorways still in the future, the 1950s provided the railways with an Indian summer in the field of leisure travel, and in retrospect provided for millions of holidaymakers from all social classes a halcyon era when it remained the natural choice to travel on holiday by train.

7
Special Passenger Traffic

It appears that some years ago a witness observed that he had on a certain occasion examined the pages of "Bradshaws's guide" for some twenty minutes; whereupon the judge declared that the evidence of such a person must not be relied upon – that he was a fit subject for a commission *de lunatico inquirendo*.

F. S. Williams, *Our Iron Roads*, 1883.

For generations of railway passengers the word *Bradshaw* was synonymous with railway timetables. The first monthly edition of *Bradshaw's Railway Guide* was issued in December 1841 and continued, with only minor changes of name, to provide railway travellers with an up-to-date account 'of the times of arrival and departure of the trains of every railway in Great Britain' until the last issue in June 1961. But reading a Bradshaw's was never the easiest of tasks and led to the appearance of several guides offering a simpler compendium of timetables, notably the *ABC* (*Alphabetical Railway Guide*) sold under the maxim 'Easy as ABC'. Despite these guides, however, comprehending the timetable remained for many passengers the most perplexing aspect of railway travel, the state of the art admirably summed up in Oscar Wilde's quip: 'I would sooner lose a train by the *ABC* than catch it by *Bradshaw*'.

But not all trains appeared in the public timetables, nor indeed the working timetables used by those who actually ran the trains. These were special trains; special not because of the types of passengers carried, but for the simple reason that they ran as extra services. In essence there were three categories of train working which fell under this title, each very different in purpose and character: excursion/special-party trains; trains operated for the military authorities conveying troops and other members of the armed forces; and Royal Trains conveying the Monarch and members of the Royal Family. Light engine and empty coaching stock movements also constituted special workings, but because they were run for reasons of operating convenience and without a

RESERVATION OF SEATS IN EXPRESS TRAINS.

For the convenience of Passengers, seats can be reserved at PADDINGTON STATION and at Auxiliary Ticket Agencies in London in certain of the principal trains starting from Paddington on week days.

A limited number of seats can also be reserved at certain other stations in some of the principal trains to Paddington on week days.

A charge of 1s. 6d. per seat is made for this service. Application for reserved seats must be received by **4.0 p.m.** on the day prior to that for which the seats are required.

SEATS CANNOT BE RESERVED BY TELEPHONE.
APPLICATIONS FOR RESERVED SEATS ARE NOT ACCEPTED ON SUNDAYS.

RESTAURANT CARS.

Restaurant Cars are provided on certain Through Express Trains, as shown in the Train Time Tables. (IN SOME CASES FOR A PORTION OF THE JOURNEY ONLY.)

Restaurant Car facilities will not be available on some of the duplicated portions of certain trains on which Restaurant Cars are usually provided, and during Holiday Periods the Restaurant Cars are subject to cancellation.

Passengers desiring meals in the Cars should obtain Seat Tickets from the Conductor who will inform passengers when the meals are ready and direct them to their seats in the cars.

THE SERVICE IS LIMITED, AND THE SUPPLY OF MEALS CANNOT BE GUARANTEED.
Passengers travelling in Slip Carriages cannot obtain access to Restaurant Cars.

TARIFF (Great Western Company's Cars).

BREAKFAST.—À la carte (see separate tariff).   DINNER.—Table d'Hôte .. .. 3s. 6d.
LUNCHEON.—Table d'Hôte .. .. 3s. 6d.   TEA.—À la carte (see separate tariff).

The above prices are subject to alteration without notice.

SERVICE CHARGE.—A service charge in lieu of gratuities will be added to all bills (except cigars, cigarettes, tobacco and confectionery).

ALL THE ABOVE ARRANGEMENTS ARE SUBJECT TO ALTERATION WITHOUT NOTICE.

RESTAURANTS.

PADDINGTON STATION. A large Dining Room is available on No. 1 Departure Platform in which Breakfast, Luncheon, Tea, Dinner and Supper are served. A Quick Lunch Bar is adjacent, at which Snacks and Iced and Hot Drinks can be obtained.

BRISTOL (Temple Meads)
CARDIFF (General)
EXETER (St. David's)
NEWPORT
READING
SWINDON
Restaurants are provided at these Stations, where meals are served at popular prices.

SLEEPING CARS.

LIMITED SLEEPING CAR ACCOMMODATION is provided on the undermentioned Trains:—

Week Nights.

FIRST CLASS ONLY.
9.50 p.m. Paddington to Penzance.
11.50 p.m. Paddington to Plymouth (North Road).
8.40 p.m. Penzance to Paddington.

FIRST AND THIRD CLASS.
9.25 p.m. (Saturday nights only) Paddington to Neyland.
1.0 night (Saturday nights excepted) Paddington to Carmarthen.
8.32 p.m. Carmarthen to Paddington.

Sunday Nights.

FIRST CLASS ONLY.
9.50 p.m. Paddington to Penzance.
11.50 p.m. Paddington to Plymouth (North Road).
8.40 p.m. Penzance to Paddington.

FIRST AND THIRD CLASS.
1.0 night Paddington to Carmarthen
6.20 p.m. Neyland to Paddington.

On arrival at Paddington passengers may remain in the Cars until 8.0 a.m.

SLEEPING BERTH CHARGES :—1st Class, 21s. per person in addition to the 1st Class Fare.
3rd Class, 8s. 8d. per person in addition to the 3rd Class Fare.

Children (including infants under 3 years of age) occupying separate sleeping berths are subject to the full sleeping berth fee in addition to half the adult fare.

Application for Sleeping Berths should specify class, number required, and whether for Lady or Gentleman, or for both.

Passengers who book Sleeping Berths and fail to use them will be required to pay the Sleeping Berth charge unless notice of cancellation is given to the Company before 4.0 p.m. on the date for which the berths are booked.

Each car is provided with lavatory accommodation. The berths in First Class Sleeping Cars are furnished with sheets, blankets and pillows, and in the Third Class with rug and pillow.

An Attendant accompanies the Cars and will supply tea and biscuits at a charge of 6d. per person to Sleeping Car Passengers en route.

Dogs will not be permitted to be taken into the Sleeping Cars.

Baths and Dressing Rooms for Ladies and Gentlemen are available at Paddington Station (near the centre of No. 1 Platform).

Breakfast can be obtained from 7.30 a.m. in the Restaurant of the G.W. Royal Hotel, Paddington.

RESERVATION OF SEATS IN TRAINS AND BERTHS IN SLEEPING CARS OR VESSELS.
For conditions, see page 161.

ALL FARES AND CHARGES QUOTED ARE SUBJECT TO THE INCREASE
AUTHORISED BY THE MINISTER OF TRANSPORT AS FROM 1st OCTOBER, 1947

Some of the facilities for long-distance passengers advertised in the 1947 GWR timetable just prior to nationalisation.

payload of passengers they may be omitted from this survey.

The Working of Excursion Traffic

Although we have examined the social significance of the excursion train in the previous chapter, our concern here is with the planning and operating problems raised by handling what was by far the most voluminous category of special traffic. The basic principle underlying the running of special excursion trains was that they had to be accommodated within the framework of the timetable of ordinary train services.

This had been exactly the approach to special services adopted by the Liverpool & Manchester Railway. The company had found the compilation of its timetables 'one of the most intricate problems in general passenger operations' — understandable perhaps given its pioneering role in passenger operation.[1] The directors soon found that schedules needed to take account of weather conditions, season, connecting road and water services, and fluctuations in local economies. By the 1830s the timetable had settled into a fairly regular pattern of twelve return trains per day in summer, ten in winter. However, the general timetable took no account of the various special trains also run by the company. Already in the summer of 1831 extra trains were run in connection with the Newton horse races, while in later years trains were provided for the Conservative Club, the movement of troops and for pleasure seekers during the Whitsuntide holidays. All were run only with the specific authority of the directors, although they seem to have posed few operating problems.

However, during the mid-Victorian period the growing popularity of excursion trains imposed greater strains on the operating departments of the railways. Their commercial importance and the frequent need to run over the lines of several companies brought the question of excursion trains to the fore at meetings of railway managers. These meetings, held under the auspices of the Railway Clearing House, originated with the need to formalise arrangements for the running of extra trains to London on the occasion of the Great Exhibition in 1851.[2] After several abortive attempts to agree a code of regulation for excursion traffic to the Exhibition, the managers eventually arrived at an agreement

FIRST CLASS SLEEPING BERTHS

are provided on the Night Expresses between

LONDON and **Glasgow, Edinburgh, Perth, Stranraer, Aberdeen, Inverness, Holyhead, Liverpool, Manchester.**

THIRD CLASS SLEEPING ACCOMMODATION

Third Class Sleeping Compartments comprise lying-down accommodation with four berths in each compartment (two upper and two lower). Each berth is equipped with a pillow and a rug. The number of berths is limited, and they will be allocated in order of application.

CHARGES IN ADDITION TO FARES.

	First Class.	Third Class.
To places South of Carlisle	15/9	6/6
To Carlisle and places North thereof	21/-	7/6

NIGHT TRAVEL IN COMFORT BY LMS

INTERAVAILABILITY OF TICKETS

between the **L M S, L. & N. E.** and **G.W. COMPANIES**

Passengers holding ORDINARY RETURN, TOURIST and MONTHLY RETURN TICKETS covering places served by the Lines of all three of the L M S, L. & N. E. and G.W. Companies or of any two of them (including Joint Lines owned by any two of these Companies) are allowed to travel on the RETURN journey between such places by any of the recognised routes of these Companies.

Break of journey is allowed to holders of the above-mentioned tickets at intermediate Stations on the alternative route.

WEEK-END and other descriptions of REDUCED FARE TICKETS (except DAY and HALF-DAY EXCURSION) are also available on the RETURN by the alternative route.

The interavailability indicated above also covers the use of the three Companies' recognised routes to or from London, in the case of passengers holding tickets via London, with places on the Southern Company's Line.

SEASON TICKETS (Ordinary and Traders') are interavailable for THROUGHOUT journeys between common places, and particulars can be obtained from the issuing Company.

PAYMENT OF CABIN AND BERTH FEES ON STEAMERS

The Railway and Steamship Companies concerned give notice that in the interests of the travelling public they must make the condition that for all sailings applications for sleeping berth accommodation on the steamers operating on the undermentioned routes must be accompanied by the requisite fee, and they will not effect cabin or berth reservations for sailings until the fees are paid—

Heysham and Belfast	Holyhead and Kingstown
Liverpool and Belfast	Liverpool and Dublin
Glasgow and Belfast	Liverpool and Cork
Glasgow and Londonderry	Glasgow and Dublin
Stranraer and Larne	Fishguard and Cork (Direct)

Also in the reverse direction.

Passengers booking cabins or berths and subsequently desiring to cancel the reservation are requested to give the Company concerned the following notice to this effect:—

For sailings from 6.0 p.m. to midnight (inclusive)—Not later than 10.30 a.m. on the day of sailing.

For sailings between midnight and 6.0 p.m.—Not later than 10.30 a.m. on the day previous to the day of sailing.

Unless such notice is given it is regretted that applications for the refund of fees paid cannot be entertained.

The Companies wish to emphasise that strict adherence to these conditions is essential in the interests of passengers, many of whom have been inconvenienced in the past owing to accommodation being reserved and not taken up, thereby preventing them from being able to secure vacant cabins or berths until after the steamers have sailed.

Despite the competition for passenger traffic which on some routes continued unabated between the Wars, the interavailability of tickets between the LMS, LNER and GWR (advertised here in the 1939 LMS timetable) foreshadowed the 'national' system of the nationalised railways.

stipulating the dates of the first excursions and stipulating fares on certain routes.[3]

Henceforth the general managers continued to meet on a regular basis, dealing amongst other business with excursion arrangements. In 1854, for instance, they dealt with the running of special trains to the Agricultural Exhibition; in 1857 they agreed on cheap fares to the Manchester Exhibition; in 1867 they discussed the general revision of excursion fares, agreeing where possible to increase them at the same time as abolishing the issue of first-class tickets on excursions (except to the Paris Exhibition).[4] With general policy determined, the task of implementation fell to the various passenger superintendents of the railways concerned.

In several respects the regular meetings of the superintendents at the Clearing House are more revealing of the development and organisation of special traffic than those of their superiors. While the managers worked out the general principles, the superintendents were left to thrash out the details. Generally their work fell into two broad areas; the regulation of fares and conditions of travel by special trains and the restriction, wherever possible, of unnecessary competition between the companies. Spring-time meetings were usually devoted to devising suitable arrangements for the forthcoming holiday season. For example, in April 1857 the superintendents set minimum fares for day trips by 'Scholars and Friends' during Whit week; decided to refuse any commission or discount to 'Proposers or Conductors of School Trips'; restricted the use of third-class excursion tickets between Manchester and Liverpool to the day of issue; set fares to the Manchester Exhibition; and agreed to restrict as far as possible the conveyance of excursion passengers to special excursion trains. In later years the superintendents also dealt with the arrangements for advertising excursions, regulating the appearance of notices in the press and agreeing lists of 'suitable' newspapers.[5]

By the 1860s and 1870s the superintendents were organising the running of excursions to a vast range of destinations and special events, among them the Cambridge Steeplechases, Doncaster races, Easter excursions to Dublin, Epsom races, Foresters' Fetes, the Handel Festival, Hereford Music Festival, the Horticultural Exhibition, Oddfellows' Fetes, the Paris Exhibition, Smithfield cattle shows, University boat races, Temperance Fetes and various religious conferences. But one type of excursion began to dominate proceedings during these years: cheap Saturday trips to the seaside. The superintendents were forced to devote an increasing amount of time to arranging the summer programme. In 1875, for example, the agenda of forthcoming excursions was so lengthy that a two-day meeting was insufficient to get through the business, forcing the superintendents to reconvene on two further occasions.[6] By the later 1870s the enterprise of the railways was such that it was agreed that any company intending to run an excursion should give its competitors at least three days notice before announcing it to the public.[7]

The task of translating Clearing House agreements into practice fell to the operating staffs of the various railways. Since neither public nor working timetables made provision for excursions or specials of any sort, it was not possible to make detailed arrangements until the schedules of ordinary trains were to hand. By the end of the nineteenth century the ordinary timetables were normally revised each spring and autumn. Although the services run in the previous year usually provided the basis for the new timetable, it remained a complex business: the loading and revenue earned by various train services, the emergence of new patterns of travel demand, fluctuations in local economies and seasonal variations all had to be taken into account. The timetable staff worked about three months in advance of publication, leaving little time for errors to be rectified and further amendments incorporated. Once the ordinary passenger services had been scheduled then freight, empty coach and locomotive movements could be revised accordingly, the whole coming together in the working timetable issued to the operating staff only a week or so before its introduction. It was only at this point that detailed timings for special excursions could be made and the necessary locomotives and rolling stock allocated.

The practice of organising specials only when the schedules of ordinary services were to hand was still the norm by the 1920s and 1930s. Critics argued, with some justification, that it made for a certain degree of inefficiency and inflexibility in the commercial organisation of such services. It was not unusual for trains to be allocated a departure time and pathway certain to give a late arrival at the destination. More importantly perhaps, it was difficult to give promoters of special trips detailed timings until close to the date of departure. Canvassing staff who had worked hard to bring excursion business to the passenger department could easily find their efforts undermined, as a member of the LNER management observed:

> Times cannot be quoted because the date of the trip is too far ahead, it is not certain whether the coaching stock will be available, the ordinary services are not complete and in any case the times asked for would probably clash with ordinary services. . . . In the meantime the Commercial Officer is being worried by the Canvasser for the information, and the latter is in despair at the prospect of losing the traffic. More important, the promoter is unable to proceed with his arrangements and in consequence considers alternative forms of transport for his party and vows that he will have no further business with the Railway Companies.[8]

One alternative to making provision for excursions and other specials only when the schedules of ordinary services had been arranged was to leave a provisional 'excursion' path clear for each hour of the day. This, it was argued, would have allowed the railways to quote specific times to promoters as requests for special trains came in and, where necessary, give an alternative time if the original request could not be met.

As it was railway passengers continued to suffer from late running caused by summer traffic congestion for much of the Inter-War period. High summer weekends in particular saw conditions at many of the major city termini in a state of chaos, with huge crowds of passengers waiting for both ordinary and special services destined for the seaside or country. On such occasions the railways resorted to the rostering of relief trains. However, this practice frequently resulted in staff and coaching stock being taken from normal workings at short notice. As successive relief trains were despatched on a 'follow the leader' basis the timetable tended to collapse, any delays down the line compounding the chaos and late running. For example, summer trains to the West Country were often delayed by the infamous bottleneck at Cogload Junction, five miles north of Taunton. Here trains from the North and Midlands converged with those from London before making their way to Taunton station where carriages for Ilfracombe and Minehead were detached. Despite the quadrupling of the running lines through Taunton and other modifications, traffic congestion along the GWR's West Country main line remained a problem up to the Second World War and beyond.

The chaos that sometimes accompanied summer weekend travel was a measure of the still vital role performed by the railway in leisure travel. It was a traffic which the railways themselves had deliberately set out to develop, particularly in the twentieth century – a point explored more fully in the next chapter. Such traffic was essential to their policy of maximising gross revenue in line with the overall revenue targets prescribed in the Railway Act of 1921. But the corollary of this policy, as two eminent transport historians have pointed out, was that the railways 'automatically sacrificed their net revenue since the additional expense incurred in meeting the requirements of concessionary passengers and in providing special services e.g., holiday specials, often outweighed the gain in receipts.'[9] It is also true that the delays and disruptions to passenger services on summer weekends were a source of much criticism from the public and did little to promote the image of the railways. As O. S. Nock comments of the GWR's experience: 'Holiday Traffic to the West of England, so carefully fostered over the thirty-odd years from the introduction of the Cornish Riviera Express was growing to embarrassing proportions.'[10]

Could the railways have done more to avoid such 'embarrassment'? Certainly by the later 1930s the disruptions to ordinary services at peak holiday periods were anticipated by the operating authorities and to a certain extent planned for. However, this was all done at short notice, leaving little time to advertise the changes to the public. It was in a sense an institutionalised form of chaos; perfectly intelligible to the railways themselves but incomprehensible to, and extremely frustrating for, their passengers. Perhaps some of the delays might have been avoided if the ordinary services at peak periods had been built around the needs of special traffic and not the other way round. But in our period at least this was never done. The problem was in any case not so much one of organisation, but investment in extra capacity at certain strategic points in the system. Given the highly seasonal nature of much special excursion traffic, such investment could hardly be justified knowing that for most of the year it would simply represent excess capacity. Arguably the ultimate, if drastic, 'solution' to the problems caused by extra traffic at peak holiday periods came with the post-War rise of mass motoring and the decline of the railway train as the natural medium for leisure travel.

The Railways and Special Military Traffic

Demands of war rather than the whims of peace-time pleasure seekers arguably provided the railways with a stiffer test of their ability to handle special passenger traffic. The utility of the railway in the event of war – either as a tool of defence or attack – had been recognised long before the outbreak of the First World War. In Europe, where route-marches had been a way of life (and death) for generations of soldiers, the advantages of a system of railways for the movement of troops, munitions and supplies were soon realised. In 1846 a whole army corps of twelve thousand Prussian soldiers was able to mass at Cracow using two lines of railway. During the 1840s and 1850s there were several more European demonstrations of the value of the railway in military operations, including the British built Balaclava Railway in the Crimea. But it was during the American Civil War that the railway really demonstrated its strategic significance. By allowing the North to mount its massive attacks in Tennessee and down the Missippippi the South was broken and notice served that 'power could now be yielded by determined governments over greater distances with complete effectiveness.'[11]

In Britain it was the preservation of internal peace rather than external threat which brought the railway to the fore as an appendage of government and the military. During the Chartist disturbances of the 1840s the railways were used extensively to move troops around the country with 'unprecedented swiftness'.[12] The importance of the railway's role in maintaining internal peace was recognised in 1842 with the passing of 'An Act for the better Regulation of Railways and for the Conveyance of Troops'. Section 20 of this Act stipulated that 'Wherever it shall be necessary to move any of the officers or soldiers of Her Majesty's forces of the line . . . by any railway, the directors shall permit them with baggage, stores, arms, ammunition and other necessaries and things to be conveyed, at the usual hour of starting.'[13] The implication was the troop movements would as far as possible be conducted by ordinary train services. However, given the accoutrements mentioned in the Act and the special facilities usually required by soldiers on the move (station buildings, for instance, were often converted into temporary barrack accommodation) the traffic could hardly be deemed ordinary.

It was one thing to be able to move a few detachments to local trouble spots, quite another to turn the entire railway system to the needs of war and national defence. The strategic importance of railways in this sense began to be recognised during the 1860s and 1870s. Two pieces of legislation – the Regulation of the Forces Act, 1871 and the National Defence Act, 1888 – made provision for government control of the railways in time of war. Yet the question of how they would be managed during a national emergency remained unclear since both Acts allowed for different arrangements. Under the Act of 1871 it was assumed the railways would be worked as a single unit; the later Act merely gave to government traffic precedence over ordinary traffic, each railway remaining under independent control.

Equally unresolved by the late nineteenth century was the railway's precise role in the event of full-scale mobilisation. A plan – 'Time-tables for Special Troop Trains' – had been prepared in 1861 by the Engineer & Railway Volunteer Staff Corps (formed the previous year). However, this was a relatively crude document, made it seems without adequate information from the military as to their expectations of the railway in wartime. From a different perspective railway managers belonging to the Volunteer Staff Corps were critical of the ignorance of both government and the military towards the importance of rail transport. As one eminent railway manager observed in 1890:

> It is very much a matter of regret to me that the operations of entraining and detraining troops, horses, and guns are so unfamiliar as they are to the British soldier. These, like any other kind of operation, can be carried out in two ways – quickly and expertly, or slow and clumsily – and the difference must be entirely a matter of practice. It is, in short, a form of drill in itself, which our troops get little or no opportunity of practising.[14]

Despite these strictures, however, military thinking at this time held different priorities, admirably encapsulated in the comment of

Lord Wolseley that it was more important to accustom troops to travel at sea rather than by rail 'inasmuch as so many need to be sent on long voyages.' With the needs of far-flung empire uppermost, it was not in fact until shortly before the First World War that a more coherent state policy for the control and operation of railways in wartime began to emerge. In 1909 a full mobilisation plan was agreed between the railway companies and the War Office. Subsequently refined this plan became a detailed and serviceable document covering not just the movement of special troop trains but also the mobilisation of the Royal Naval Reserve. It was also confirmed that the railways would be managed as a single system during an emergency, a Railway Executive Committee (comprising the general managers of the twelve major companies) being formed in 1912 for the purpose. This was supplemented by a Communications Board (composed of representatives from the Home Office, Admiralty, War Office, Board of Trade, Railway Executive Committee and headed by the Quartermaster General of the Forces) created in 1913 to enable an exchange of views on arrangements for future emergencies.[15]

In essence this was the state of organisation for the mobilisation and subsequent movement of military forces in Great Britain upon the declaration of war with Germany on 4 August 1914. During the first two weeks of hostilities the railways were to play an instrumental part in mobilisation: on the GWR 632 special troop trains were run during this period; on the LNWR 550; with other companies handling traffic of similar proportions. However, the greatest flow of traffic in these early weeks was on the lines of the LSWR, as the first members of the British Expeditionary Force travelled to Southampton for despatch to France. By the end of August 1914 over 118,000 military personnel carried in 670 trains had been dealt with at Southampton.[16] As the Western Front was established and the pattern of war developed into dispiriting attrition the railways at home became involved in the steady movement of troops to and from the Front.

Being the railways closest to the war the southern systems played a strategic role. Victoria was one of the main London stations for despatching and receiving troops. Leave traffic was particularly heavy, with special leave trains arriving from Folkestone regularly during the winter of 1914–15. Later as many as twelve special troop

146

trains a day ran each way on this route, with a further two between Victoria and Dover. The SECR's lines also saw heavy traffic. According to Alan Jackson, Charing Cross station was in constant use by government ministers and military leaders making their way to and from France. Such passengers often made use of a special train code-named *Imperial A*. Running non-stop on a cleared path this train made 283 journeys to the coast during the course of the war. Charing Cross also despatched a daily special to Folkestone conveying military staff officers.[17]

On each of the major railways special military departments, formed from civilian railway clerical staff, dealt with all army and navy traffic. Upon receiving instructions from the Command authorities it was the task of these departments to procure suitable rolling stock commensurate with weight and gauge limitations, provide pilot drivers with appropriate route knowledge, and draw up timetables for departures and arrivals at the various bases. It was a complex task, sometimes made more difficult during the early months of the war by the actions of local officers who took it as their right to order up at short notice special trains. Despite these problems, however, the railway departments coped valiantly with the pressures. 'So efficient did the railway "military" men become', Edwin A. Pratt concluded in his classic study of the wartime railways, 'that notwithstanding the complications involved . . . anything in the nature of a hitch was, so far as can be ascertained, practically unknown during the War.'[18]

In addition to the demands upon railway resources made by the War Office, the railways also had to cope with the quite different requirements of the Admiralty. The Grand Fleet was based at Scapa Flow in the Orkneys, the nearest port of embarkation being Scrabster Harbour near Thurso. Thus, for naval forces long journeys by train were a necessary part of movements to and from the Fleet. As the war progressed and traffic increased the running of ad hoc specials to the far north of Scotland began to impose a severe strain on the railways; the Highland Railway in particular struggled to cope with a vast increase in traffic passing through Inverness. Travelling conditions were far from ideal – overcrowded trains, poor connections with ordinary services and cases of antagonism between civilian passengers and sailors.

To combat these problems transport administration at Inverness was improved with a staff of around 550 dedicated to the requirements of Admiralty traffic. In addition the dependence upon irregular special workings was reduced with the inauguration early in 1917 of a daily train – the 'Naval Special' – running each way between London and Thurso. This departed Euston at 6pm (3pm in winter to allow a daylight embarkation at Thurso) and reached Thurso at 3.33pm the following day – 21hr 30min for a run of 717 miles. The train was invariably a heavy one, fourteen coaches being the usual complement, and was timed to provide connections with other services at key points en route. Given the length of journey and the exigencies of wartime operations, the Euston-Thurso special earned a remarkable record for its punctuality. Even so, travel by the special must have been an arduous experience – there were no buffet facilities, the men having to rely on food supplied by volunteer workers at the various stopping points.[19]

One final variant of First World War military traffic remains to be considered, the ambulance train. Only a few weeks after the euphoric departure of the Expeditionary Force the first casualties were arriving back at Southampton docks and being conveyed to hospital in special trains of ambulance vehicles. For the duration of this most cruel of conflicts – the first mechanised war in history – hundreds of thousands of wounded servicemen were to follow in their wake, a grim and tragic contrast to the departure when, in the words of Wilfred Owen's poem 'The Send-Off', men had

> sang their way
> To the Siding-shed,
> And lined the train with faces grimly gay.

The need for ambulance trains had been anticipated before 1914 – valuable experience in their construction and operation being gained during the Boer War. Plans for the ambulance trains constructed for the 1914–18 War were prepared by the LNWR in consultation with the medical authorities of the War Office. Twelve complete trains were ordered, each comprising nine vehicles converted from existing coaching stock and providing berths for sitting and stretcher cases, a pharmacy, day and sleeping accommodation for medical staff, and kitchen and dining facilities. As the number of wartime casualties mounted – in one week alone during July 1916 47,000 sick and wounded were landed at British ports – so additions and modifications to the ambulance train fleet were made. Eventually there were twenty specialised ambulance trains available, supplemented by a range of vehicles which could be pressed into service in emergencies. At any one time the railways could provide transportation for over 8,000 casualties (excluding accommodation on naval and overseas ambulance trains).

Wartime casualties were distributed to hospitals nationwide. Admiralty ambulance trains in particular ran over long distances. A regular service of four trains operated a circular route between Edinburgh and Chatham taking in the major East Coast ports as well as Plymouth and Gosport. The efficiency with which the railways handled wartime casualties contrasted sharply with the confusion and ineptitude in other areas of the war. It was not unknown for casualties to reach their point of destination in Britain within twenty four hours of receiving their wounds. During the course of the war the railways were to carry over 2.5 million sick and wounded servicemen by special ambulance trains.[20]

The verdict on the railways' performance during the First World War is generally favourable. Despite the strains of heavy military traffic, increased freight and civilian passenger traffic and the depletion of resources, the railways struggled on valiantly with minimal dislocation. The experience provided something of a blueprint for action during the Second World War. As in the years 1914–18 the railways were to make a prodigious contribution to the war effort, carrying a vastly increased quantity of freight and civilian traffic supplemented by millions of military personnel. Nevertheless, in several respects the tasks the railways were expected to perform and the conditions in which they had to be accomplished were markedly different to those of the First World War.

In September 1939 the railways came under the authority of the Minister of Transport, responsibility for their day-to-day operation being vested in the Railway Executive Committee (REC) consisting of the General Managers of the main line companies and the London Passenger Transport Board. Among the first tasks of the REC was to organise the movement of the British Expeditionary Force to Southampton for embarkation. But this action was overshadowed by the Evacuation – 'probably the greatest controlled mass movement of human beings within so short a time

that the world had ever seen.'[21] The first evacuations of early
September 1939 took some 600,000 children, each (in theory)
neatly labelled and carrying gas mask, food and clothing, out of
London in just four days. The LMS alone carried half a million
evacuees during this period, the disruption to other services being
minimised by taking some to Watford by suburban electric where
they changed to steam trains. By the end of the war over 1.5 million
evacuees had been transported from city to countryside in 2,000
special trains.[22]

The cause of all this activity – the fear and later reality of enemy
bombing – contributed to the first major transport crisis of the war
during the winter of 1940–41. Much more than the First World
War, when bombing had been relatively limited, the strategic
importance of the railways made them a target of high priority.
Extensive damage was inflicted on railway facilities, including
stations, with large numbers of casualties among railwaymen. With
other problems caused by shortages of locomotives and rolling
stock and changes in the pattern of freight traffic, the government
was forced to intervene. Improvements to operating methods,
additional facilities and greater planning and coordination of
public transport ensured that the crisis did not develop into a
full-scale stoppage.[23]

Despite the bombs and the heavy wartime traffic the railways and
their stations managed to maintain essential services. Station staff
in particular coped with intense demands on facilities, especially for
refreshments, from both military and civilian travellers. Railway
refreshment rooms were frequently the scene of marathon efforts by
volunteers, often working round the clock to satisfy a seemingly
endless demand for food and drink. But the free canteens for
servicemen established on railway stations in some cases provided
an apposite comment on army rations, as the railway historian
Hamilton Ellis remembered:

> One recalls a very weary and very hungry soldier truly counting his
> pennies at Preston, and the way his face lit up when a nice WVS lady
> told him he could have what he liked; there was nothing to pay there.
> At the same time, the free canteens could be abused. Men in much
> less need would sometimes stuff themselves at Preston and then
> throw their official rations under the carriages at Crewe.[24]

For civilian passengers the war brought considerable changes to travelling conditions. Long queues, withdrawn services, late running and heavy overcrowding became routine features of wartime trains. Travel at night was especially tedious: long hours of slow progress in carriages with blinds down and only partially lit by dim blue bulbs. Despite the rigours and an intensive government campaign against unnecessary civilian travel, large numbers continued to travel. By 1944 total passenger mileage was 68 per cent higher than it had been in 1938, while available carriage stock had actually decreased by 8.6 per cent.[25] But perhaps even more than the First World War, the really heroic efforts of the railways were reserved for the running of huge numbers of special military trains. Constant movements of troops to ports, camps and on leave brought a vast increase in special traffic to the railways. But at certain times – notably the Dunkirk evacuation and the preparations for D-Day – the railways were forced to intensify still further their efforts.

The evacuation from Dunkirk in 1940 took some 319,000 troops to the various reception ports along the south-east coast. Their subsequent movement to inland reception centres by special trains produced arguably 'the most wonderful emergency service ever organised in the history of British railways.'[26] The burden of operation fell heavily on the Southern Railway, but all four companies were involved together forming a pool of 186 rakes of coaches for the purpose. In addition there were extensive train movements from the south-west ports carrying troops evacuated from the Biscayan area of France.

The build-up to D-Day in 1944 saw much more extensive movements in the reverse direction as Allied troops, including large numbers of Americans, were massed at strategic points along the South Coast in readiness for the assault on the Normandy beaches. This traffic reached a peak during early June when in a six day period the railways carried 99,000 troops in 271 special trains.[27] The success of the invasion brought little relief to over-worked railway staff. As one GWR fireman on the Didcot–Southampton route later recalled:

we were very busy running troop trains from Newbury and Sutton Scotney to Southampton Docks, returning with the empty coaches for a second and third trip before being released. Then, as the advance built up, we had train-loads of German prisoners for either Newbury or Banbury.[28]

By the end of the war the railways had run a total of 538,559 special trains of which just under half were troop trains; a monumental effort given the depletion of manpower and resources. But the price of this effort was high. The railways entered the post-war period facing a massive backlog of maintenance and renewals and with a public image badly tarnished by the discomforts, delays and overcrowding associated with wartime travel.

Railways and Royal Passengers

Troop trains to the battlefield, or the sad procession of returning trains carrying the war weary and wounded formed a stark contrast to the third category of special traffic, royal passengers. The first railway journey by a reigning British monarch was made by Queen Victoria between Slough, then the nearest station to Windsor, and London Paddington on 13 June 1842. Although the GWR had been given only forty eight hours notice, the company was able to provide a royal saloon built two years earlier in anticipation of just such an event. Drawn by one of the company's new 7ft singles with Brunel and Gooch on the footplate, the journey went without hitch taking just twenty five minutes.[29] 'Thereafter', Ellis informs us, 'she was to use the Great Western line between London and Windsor for the rest of her days, even unto the conveyance of her funeral long years on, in 1901.'[30] But the GWR was by no means the only railway company favoured by Victoria. Journeys to various residences, especially her favourite retreats at Frogmore on the Isle of Wight and Balmoral in Scotland, and an extensive itinerary of pleasure seeking trips and official visits ensured regular forays by railway train.

The decision to accord the railway royal patronage was hardly as momentous as is sometimes suggested. Indeed, in the case of the Queen's first essay in Anglo-Scottish railway travel in 1848, the train had been resorted to only because dense fog had prevented a planned return from Balmoral by sea. It is true that royal patronage may have stimulated extra traffic for, as Jack Simmons suggests, such was the cult of royalty and sentimental attachment to Victoria that the public followed even to the places she visited.[31] However, had Victoria set her face against the by then not so novel form of travel, it is hard to see how either the railways or travelling public would have suffered. By 1842 Prince Albert was in any case already a confirmed railway traveller, having used the GWR route between Paddington and Slough on several previous occasions. While the railways no doubt welcomed the prestige accorded by royal patronage and any extra traffic it may have stimulated, the safe and expeditious operation of royal specials was not without its problems.

Whereas other special traffic had to be accommodated within the normal schedules of timetabled trains, in the case of royal specials the ordinary service was temporarily suspended. Safety, of course, was a paramount consideration. In addition to despatching a pilot engine in advance of the royal train, facing points were normally bolted, level crossings closed and no trains allowed to follow for at least fifteen minutes. On the LNWR it was normal practice for 'the whole staff of platelayers, porters, police, etc. . . . to guard the line during the Royal Progess.'[32] When the monarch travelled north on the GNR, the general manager issued detailed instructions stipulating when, where and for how long the royal train was to stop. In addition GNR royal trains were accompanied by the company's carriage foreman and two fitters whose duty was 'to alight immediately the train stops . . . examine and supply every axle box, reporting . . . their condition at every stopping place.' Marshalled at either end of the train were brakevans on which two guards and two fitters were to act as a constant lookout on each side of the train.[33]

Railway managements were prepared to go to extraordinary, almost paranoic, lengths to ensure that the monarch was insulated from the realities of travel by train. G. P. Neele, the man in charge of the LNWR's royal train, recalled one incident in 1885 when the train was parked for the night at Wigan:

> While the examination of the vehicles was being carried out as usual with all possible quietude to give an undisturbed night's rest to the Royal Travellers, I was much annoyed to hear one of the up mails approaching at the full speed which such trains can display in passing along the falling gradient at that place, and, in addition to the roar of

the train, the driver, for reasons of his own, opened his whistle and kept it going shrilly as he passed along the line close to the stationary train.

Fearing a royal reprimand for the incident Neele resolved to prevent any repetition in the future and henceforth included an order that 'no train, mail or express, should be allowed to pass through either Wigan or Oxenholme, during the time the Royal train might be standing there.'[34]

Royal specials, which became an accepted part of life for both monarch and railways during the nineteenth century, certainly did not come to an end with the death of Victoria in 1901. Ironically the almost funereal progress of royal trains during Victoria's reign was conspicuously absent on the occasion of her funeral. Because of various delays to the royal cortege the train – provided on this sombre occasion by the LBSC – was forced to travel at a decidedly unstately pace. In a sense it was symbolic of a new era in the running of royal specials: freed from Victoria's sentimental attachment to certain vehicles the railways began to provide more modern and sumptuous accommodation able to travel at higher speeds.

Nevertheless, with the First World War the age of great royal train specials had arguably come to an end. Royal trains continued to operate – as they still do today – but the journey of the monarch by rail was no longer a 'royal progress' in the Victorian sense. Edward VIII, for example, who disliked his legacy of railway vehicles, tended to use his official saloon in the mode of a business car rather than a sumptuous conveyance. For shorter distance travel, especially on the Southern lines, it became normal practice for the monarch to travel in standard coaching stock, such as Pullman vehicles. Many of the royal saloons of the various companies survived until nationalisation and beyond, but in essence they had outlived the age of monarchy and empire which had produced them.

8
Promoting the Railway Travel Habit

Instead of letting the public come to the railway only when compelled to use the train service, railway companies now urge it by every possible means to use their services, creating reasons for people to travel by train and offering every kind of inducement to do so.

Railway Service Journal, March 1933

Publicity before 1914

For much of the nineteenth century the attitude of the railway companies towards the marketing of passenger train services was conditioned by their virtually unchallenged position in the market for personal travel. Confident of the railway's appeal as a passenger carrier, the early companies' approach to advertising was small scale and somewhat haphazard. Regular train services and fares were brought to the attention of the public through the official 'timebooks' sold at station booking offices, the commercially produced guides such as *Bradshaws* and *ABC,* and periodic announcements in the press. Special excursion trains and other cheap travel facilities required greater publicity, usually achieved through the issue of handbills giving details about destinations, times and fares and notices in local newspapers.

Beyond this, little serious thought was given to promoting their services and facilities. Ironically railway property was used extensively by other business enterprises for advertising purposes. Bridges, linesides, stations and approach roads were soon covered in a plethora of enamel signs and posters extolling the virtues of a vast range of wares.[1] It was not until the later Victorian period that the railways themselves began to see the advantages of promoting their travel services and facilities in the same manner as Fry's Chocolate, Pear's Soap or Camp Coffee. As one reviewer of early railway publicity commented, the companies were 'innocent of the effect which well planned and executed publicity has on the public mind.'[2]

The approach of the GWR was typical of many. An advertising agent was employed on a commission basis in the early years of the company, but his services seem to have been dispensed with well before 1870. By this time the company relied on handbills and the usual press advertisments, responsibility for which rested on an advertising clerk in the general manager's office assisted by two bill inspectors (divisional offices inserting their own advertisements in the local press). Like most railway advertisements, these tended to be crowded with detail, much of it unnecessary, while handbills tended to be printed on 'flimsy coloured paper' with such a conglomeration of type 'as to repel the most eager of potential passengers.'[3] Until the creation of a separate advertising department in 1886, GWR publicity, according to R. Burdett Wilson's informative study, was dominated by 'conservatism and a lack of enterprise'.[4]

Despite these criticisms, however, it should not be inferred that the railways were entirely oblivious of the need to promote in wider terms their services and facilities. Investment in ancillary passenger facilities suggests that some railways at least were conscious of the need to assist where possible the development of traffic. Railway hotels, for example, did much to promote tourist traffic on the railways. As Jack Simmons has argued in an important exploratory study of railways and tourism, the move into the hotel business was seen primarily as a means of promoting new passenger traffic rather than an invesment in its own right.[5] While the majority of railway hotels – by 1913 there were 112 in the UK – were to be found in the larger cities, a few were located in the countryside. The GWR opened the Tregenna Castle Hotel in Cornwall – a converted country house – in 1878, the Midland the Heysham Tower in 1904; while in Scotland several railway hotels were linked with golf courses, notably at Cruden Bay, Dornoch, Turnberry and Gleneagles.[6]

Recognition of the contribution made by tourism to passenger traffic led most of the leading companies to appoint travel agents to develop this branch of their business. The firm of Thomas Cook – already by mid-nineteenth century with an unrivalled experience in the organisation of tours at home and abroad – was soon closely associated with the Midland Railway; the LNWR and LSWR with Henry Gaze of Southampton; the MS&L with John Dawson.[7]

Overseas agents were also appointed by several companies. In the 1890s the LNWR agent in New York was to supply transatlantic passengers with information outlining the advantages of the LNWR route. At Queenstown the company had another agent responsible for extending 'a personal sympathy, arranging trains to Dublin, or forwarding messages for accommodation at Liverpool, should the voyager decide to continue to that port.'[8] By this time the LNWR, in competition with the LSWR, was advertising special boat trains to and from Euston connecting with the Atlantic steamers of Cunard and the White Star Line.

The LNWR and the South Eastern & Chatham were also to play a pioneering role in attracting French and other European tourists to Britain. To overcome what a contemporary reviewer perceived as the prediliction of the average Gaul for his own country, the LNWR opened offices in the Boulevard des Italiens in Paris, sending a member of the general manager's staff to take up the post of continental representative. Simultaneously the company made a valiant assault on the insularity of their English speaking staff: 'Guides or interpreters are pressed into service and [company] hotels are provided with a sufficient proportion of servants to whom "the French of Paris" is not altogether unknown.'[9]

As efforts to promote tourist and other leisure traffic gained momentum, several companies began to appreciate more fully the value of advertising. Gradually publicity policy became more enterprising. By the later 1870s the LNWR was issuing booklets outlining its 'Programme of Two Monthly Tickets' which contained maps of railways in North Wales, Ireland, Scotland and the Lake District, and a list of tourist tickets with their conditions of use.[10] The NER also acquired a reputation for imaginative use of publicity with its promotion of travel to the seaside resorts of Yorkshire. Recognition of the valuable role of publicity in promoting travel led to the establishment of specific publicity departments. By 1914 several of the leading companies had taken this step leading the *Jubilee of the Railway News* to observe: 'The publicity department is . . . of quite recent growth, the youngest of the special service branches of railway administration, the newest extension created by present-day conditions of life.'[11]

During the 1890s the GWR's new publicity department began to produce the company's programme of seasonal excursion arrangements in booklet form. In addition to train services this included notes on 'principal places of attraction' served by the railway. A London publisher was also authorised to produce the first in what was to prove a long series of booklets giving information on hotels and other holiday accommodation in GWR territory. By 1905 the *Great Western Railway: Farmhouse, Seaside, Country Lodgings, Boarding Houses and Hotels* ran to 200 pages, its popularity inspiring the company to publish its own book – *Holiday Haunts* – a year later.[12]

By the turn of the century the railways were also beginning to supplement their traditional forms of 'informative' advertising with a more creative approach using the new medium of pictorial posters. Unfortunately, some of the earliest railway posters were rather undistinguished, tending towards a conservative 'pretty picture' style with the emphasis firmly on the scenic splendour of the countryside served by the company. Most possessed neither atmosphere nor visual impact, but there were some exceptions such as the NER's 'Alice in Holidayland' designed to boost traffic to the Yorkshire coast and John Hassall's now legendary 'Skegness is so bracing' design for the GNR. Poster campaigns were sometimes linked to the issue of illustrated booklets promoting the holiday regions and resorts served by the railway. Thus, the NER posters invited passengers to write for a free copy of 'Alice in Holidayland', a booklet containing a 'New Version in Picture and Verse of a story beloved by children.'

Not all poster and booklet campaigns were aimed at stimulating tourist or holiday traffic. 'Where to Live', a booklet produced by the GNR, was one of several aimed at the suburban passenger. Nonetheless, the importance of leisure in publicity policy was reflected in the slogans adopted by several of the pre-Grouping companies: the 'Holiday Line' – GWR; the 'Sunshine Line' – LBSC; 'The Golfers' Line – GSWR. How much these and other similar campaigns contributed to the growth of traffic is difficult to assess. But there is little doubt that the more successful of them helped to create new and often lasting images of railway companies and the towns and regions they served.

Notwithstanding the efforts of the main line companies, it was the London Underground Group – forerunner of London Transport – which established itself as the clear leader in the field of

Commencing on the 16th

September, a private secretarial service for the benefit of business travellers will be provided on 'The Comet' express trains between London and Manchester from Mondays to Fridays.

You will be able to go along to a specially equipped office compartment and in complete privacy dictate letters and memoranda or give copy material to a competent secretary. She will produce the subject matter, neatly typed, for collection later on the journey.

WHERE IS THE TRAIN SECRETARY?

Leaving Euston, the Secretary's office is towards the front of the train.

Leaving Manchester, it is towards the rear.

The compartment will be labelled 'Train Secretary'

TIMES OF 'THE COMET'

Depart	EUSTON	9.45 am	MANCHESTER *London Road*	5.45 pm
Due	MANCHESTER *London Road*	1.20 pm	EUSTON	9.25 pm

CHARGES

(Dictation and typing or copy-typing, including provision of notepaper if required)

Per Octavo sheet 1/-

Per Quarto sheet 2/6

Per Foolscap sheet 3/6

The importance of the mass travel market to the railways' fortunes did not prevent continued attempts in the twentieth century to fete the relatively small number of Pullman and first-class passengers. In this advertisement it is the business executive who, it is hoped, will decide to travel by train because of the availability of a 'Train Secretary'.

pre-War railway poster design and deployment. Following the appointment of Albert Stanley (later Lord Ashfield) as general manager in 1907, publicity assumed a pivotal role in the Group's attempts to compete more successfully with bus and tram services. Responsibility for publicity was given to Frank Pick, a young recruit to the organisation who had won a reputation as a particularly vocal critic of existing advertising policy. From the start, as Christian Barman's biography makes clear, Pick began to chart new and imaginative directions in railway publicity. Leading exponents of the new art of poster design such as John Hassall, Fred Taylor, Gregory Brown, E. MacKnight Kauffer and Ernest Jackson, were commissioned by Pick to produce a series of bold and visually stimulating designs to reinforce themes in the Underground's contribution to London life.[13]

The first artist commissioned by Pick was John Hassall whose poster 'No Need to Ask a P'liceman' cleverly combined a map of the Underground with some humorous figures to present the concept of an underground system. Subsequent posters ranged over a wide variety of subjects, sometimes in humorous mood at other times serious. However, Pick's contribution to railway publicity was not so much in his choice of posters, inspired though it often was, but in their deployment. To heighten their impact Pick began to sweep away the jumble of posters and advertisements found at many Underground stations, replacing it with an ordered display. At the same time Pick began to develop a new design for station name signs. Red discs incorporating station names and set at the eye level of seated passengers foreshadowed the famous red ring which became the symbol of the Underground during the 1920s. Under Pick's influence, the ambience of the modern Underground had begun to emerge.[14]

However, despite these pioneering steps into the world of 'creative' advertising', before 1914 informative advertising of the type long practised by the railways continued to dominate the work of the new publicity departments. Their task was to keep the public informed by traditional methods: the issue of public timebooks, timetable folders and hanging cards; the exhibition of time sheets, programmes of local and national events, and fare tables on stations; press announcements of forthcoming excursions; and the production and display of company maps. Public timebooks and sheets changed little in style before 1914. More enterprising were the small timetable folders which were cheap to produce and easy to distribute. More readable than the full timetable these folders also helped to reduce the amount of time spent by station staff dealing with train enquiries.

Meanwhile the press continued to be a vital medium for railway advertising. Notices of special trains, cheap fares and train times appeared regularly in the press throughout the pre-1914 period. As Wilson comments of the GWR's approach to newspaper advertising: 'The smaller, non-displayed advertisements inserted week after week in hundreds of local papers, usually in the same position so that readers would know where to find them, remained the backbone of Great Western press advertising.'[15] Most railway companies seem to have accepted the utility of long-established patterns of press advertising without seriously questioning the relationship of results to costs. Certainly the propaganda value of the press was little exploited, if at all understood, during this period. It was to take a world war and the onset of a new, often hostile, commercial environment to force the railways into a reappraisal of this and other aspects of their publicity policy.

Between the Wars: New Images

The First World War brought a temporary halt to the development of railway publicity. Posters enticing people to travel were replaced by simple, direct messages conveying government information on the needs of a nation in crisis. But the period was not without some advance. On the Underground, for instance, Pick continued his progressive approach to posters, commissioning a leading American artist, MacKnight Kauffer, to produce a series of striking posters portraying various London landscapes.[16] Nonetheless, it was not until the early 1920s that the railways began to turn their attention to publicity matters again. They did so in conditions very different to those which had spawned the first stirrings of creative advertising before the war.

With the grouping of the main line companies in 1923 attention was focussed as much on the need to evoke a distinctive public image for the new and unfamiliar railway organisations as the perennial need to inform and attract potential passengers. In

RAILWAY UNDERTAKING

Touter. 'Going by train, Sir?' *Passenger*. 'M? Eh? Yes.'
Touter. 'Allow me, then, to give you one of my cards, Sir.'
(Reproduced by permission of *Punch* and by courtesy of the Lancashire Library,
Blackburn district).

addition, it was to become apparent during the twenties and thirties that the railways were no longer able to take their dominant position in the transport market for granted. As the *Railway Service Journal* (organ of clerical, administrative and supervisory staff) observed in 1930:

> Until comparatively recently the railway was for all practical purposes the only means of transit. Passengers and goods had perforce to travel by rail and the railway industry occupied itself solely with the production of efficient transport. With the coming of the motor vehicle as an alternative means of transit all this has changed, and the railway companies have to go out to seek business instead of it coming to them automatically.[17]

In this changing commercial environment the railways returned to some of the approaches to publicity tentatively explored before the war. Creative advertising in particular, was used extensively often with considerable effect. The LMS and LNER set the pace by using the work of leading artists and designers. In the mid-1920s the LMS was the first railway company to commission a number of leading Royal Academicians to provide an imposing, if orthodox, series of poster designs. More progressive perhaps were some of the posters adopted by the LNER under the influence of W. M. Teasdale, the company's advertising chief. A number of leading artists were retained during this period, producing several memorable designs in Cubist and Art Deco styles. Against the LNER material, the posters produced by both the GWR and SR were somewhat staid, although several designs by Frank Newbold did much to enliven the GWR scene during the 1930s.

The main line companies shared with their forebears a strong interest in promoting holiday and tourist traffic. The GWR, for instance, often shared with town councils advertising expenses – a factor which may in part explain the company's conservative approach to poster design.[18] All the railways produced an extensive 'holiday' literature containing details of train services, ancillary facilities and a glossy portrait of the regions and resorts they served. Thus, an LMS booklet of the mid-twenties proclaimed the virtues of the 'Shakespeare, Washington, Franklin, Bunyan and Cowper Counties' and included details of thirty three hotels owned and managed by the company. The Southern, often in intense competition with the GWR for holiday traffic to Devon and Cornwall, issued an evocative booklet 'West Country Holidays'. Written by S. P. B. Mais the reputation and romance of the Southern's multi-portioned Atlantic Coast Express 'To Glorious Devon and North Cornwall' figured prominently. The period also saw the appearance of publicity material aimed consciously at the needs of foreign tourists to Britain. 'Touring Britain', produced by the LNER, promised 'to make the pleasure of touring Britain ample and memorable', always assuming of course that the visitor travelled by LNER.[19]

Clever use of imagery might serve a variety of purposes. For example, the Metropolitan Railway's series of booklets 'Country Walks in Metroland' were ostensibly aimed at the city dweller in search of a day's peace in the countryside. The third in the series promised to take the walker through:

> some of the most intimate recesses of the Chiltern Hills . . . into a score of romantic villages, and half-a-dozen little country towns – such as the Chalfonts, Amersham, Wendover, Chesham, and the Missendens. They will take him into parks . . . to places of historic interest and haunts of ancient peace, to grey churches, to famous view points, to spreading commons, to a multitude of out-of-the way nooks and corners, where the life of the country goes on serene and sweet, unspoilt by the changes which have overwhelmed the countryside nearer town.[20]

All very compelling, but should it not be appreciated just how close such idyllic surroundings were to 'London's streaming roar' and Metropolitan line stations the booklet ended:

> Why not live in Metroland? Have you ever realised the joy of living in the country, the pleasure of rural surroundings and bracing air? . . . In Metroland – London's nearest countryside – you will find all you can reasonably ask. It has character and charm, variety and interest. There are houses ready to live in and building land ripe for development. The train service is unrivalled; the Season Ticket Rates are low.[21]

Despite the progress made in the field of creative advertising, the press remained the principal medium for railway publicity. The GWR, for instance, regularly advertised its special and cheap trains in about 250 newspapers each week.[22] On the strength of press advertising alone the LMS claimed it had sold over 30,000 holiday contract tickets during their first season of use. In another celebrated incident an incorrect time for an LMS special was inserted in the press, 300 people turning up 'obviously all attracted by an advertisment which appeared once only.'[23]

Press advertising was occasionally enlivened by incorporating slogans and logos which appeared simultaneously in other mediums. For example, in a major campaign launched by the LNER shortly before the Second World War, 'Meet the Sun on the East Coast' and a sun logo figured prominently on posters, handbills, booking office windows, road vehicles, in the literature produced by the resorts themselves, in the company's press advertising, and even on sets of stamps sold to local authorities, hotels and boarding houses.[24] The Southern Railway's publicity people also attempted to promote an association between holidays full of sunshine and the company's services. The slogan 'South for Sunshine' and the famous poster portraying a little boy on the platform end at Waterloo gazing up to a driver on the footplate with the words 'I'm taking an early holiday cos I know summer comes soonest in the South', were but two examples of the Southern's sun oriented publicity.

If posters, booklets and the press formed the mainstay of publicity between the Wars, the period was not without innovation in other mediums. The GWR in particular showed considerable, characteristically individualistic, enterprise: exhibitions, lectures, cinemas, jigsaw puzzles, table games, painting books, postcards, carriage pictures, competitions, radio broadcasting, window displays, menu cards, luggage labels, bookmarkers and maps were all at some stage turned to the cause of publicity and propaganda. Some of these initiatives, notably the sale of wooden jigsaws, were unique in railway publicity. The first puzzle, depicting a view of the engine Caerphilly Castle, appeared in 1924, the company selling no less than thirty thousand in the first year. By 1939, when the War stopped production, forty three different puzzles had been produced and over a million sold. After travel books they were, according to R. Burdett Wilson, held to be 'the most successful venture in what Sir Felix Pole called propaganda, that the company ever entered on.'[25]

Although the railways increasingly recognised the importance of well-mounted publicity campaigns, it was indicative of prevailing attitudes in the industry that far more effort went into countering the competition from other railways than from road transport. Nevertheless with traffic levels stagnating, if not falling in some areas, the railways gradually began to take the need to 'sell' railway services and facilities far more seriously. As competition from road transport intensified during the 1930s two joint initiatives – 'Its Quicker By Rail' and 'The Square Deal' campaign were launched to improve the industry's public image and boost staff morale. The companies also made a start inculcating staff with the importance of marketing their services effectively: 'Every man a salesman' noted the *Railway Service Journal* in 1930.[26] Lectures on various aspects of selling railway services were organised for railway staff in appropriate grades. Much of this effort was directed towards the freight business where personal contact with customers was frequently possible, but there was also a carryover onto the passenger side. In 1931, for instance, the LMS passenger manager told his staff 'to get in contact with as many members of the public as you can, and sell them rail travel. Give each one you meet a strong selling talk on what we are doing for them this year.'[27]

The increased concern of the LMS with the marketing of its services, reflected in the creation of the post of chief commercial manager in 1932, represented more than appointing or training salesmen. As Ashton Davies, incumbent of this post during the 1930s, observed: 'It is a much more radical business involving a new conception and changed outlook in respect of the marketing or sale of the railway companies' services and facilities.'[28] The LMS attempted to develop a much more aggressive approach to marketing, encouraging competition amongst staff by reporting their achievements in two new house journals – *Quota News* for sales performance and *On Time* for operating performance. However, the value of such strategies remained constrained by the railway companies' limited knowledge of the travel markets they served. Speaking for the LMS, though the comment had wider relevance, Davies admitted in 1939 that:

> Whilst we knew what amount of traffic (in the aggregate) originated at a particular station, and in a given district . . . beyond a distinction between first-class and third-class traffic and the separation into certain broad typical categories as to 'excursion' and 'ordinary'

Through extensive advertising (especially on stations) and with stationmasters and booking clerks as agents the Railway Passengers Assurance Company became a familiar name to generations of railway passengers.

traffic, we knew very little about what sort of traffic it really was – I mean what sort of traffic from the point of view of its revenue potentiality at varying zonal distances.[29]

To rectify its ignorance in this area the LMS instituted a survey of passenger traffic originating at its stations during the months of February and August 1932. Nevertheless, the railways tended to rely upon widely shared, but impressionistic, assumptions about the nature of travel demand which, as one recent study has argued, tended to inhibit them from making 'a greater effort to adapt the train service to the traffic.'[30] As it was the list of inducements to travel by train by the later 1930s was impressive. More sophisticated advertising and publicity policy formed only part of a wider package of measures which included cheap fares (notably monthly third-class returns at 1d per mile), holiday 'run-about' tickets, travel vouchers for business users, weekly season tickets, payment by instalment facilities and a vast range of excursion trains.

But however hard the railways attempted to improve their image and sell their services, they could not disguise the fact that the quality of train services during the period was extremely patchy. The prestige trains on the long distance routes, speeded up and heavily advertised during the 1930s, did much to bolster the railways' image. However, these improvements were often achieved at the expense of a deterioration in overall punctuality and service standards on secondary and local services.[31]

The performance of the railways during these years has been the subject of extensive criticism by both contemporaries and historians. They have been accused of a 'marked lack of enterprise in attracting traffic in the face of competition', of resting on tradition, of interpreting their legal requirements 'too rigidly', and failing to adopt 'a more scientific and commercially competitive charging policy'.[32] Against this must be set the very real difficulties facing the railways arising from structural changes in the economy, the constraints of government legislation, the rapid rise of motor transport and the absence of any clear-cut financial case for investment in modern technology.[33] Nevertheless, it remains the case that the railways under private enterprise drifted through the period without any clear or coherent strategy for the future. Beneath the gloss of publicity they remained, as the Royal Commission on Transport had argued in 1931, 'unduly

Early railway directors, usually portrayed as fat and pompous, were a favourite target for *Punch's* satire. In this cartoon two unfortunate examples are condemned to suffer the same fate as their 'ordinary' passengers (by courtesy of the Lancashire Library Blackburn District and reproduced by permission of *Punch*).

conservative' and guilty of forgetting 'the doctrine that facilities create traffic.'[34]

The Second World War denied to the railways' owners any long-term opportunity to respond to these criticisms. Their last, and ultimately futile, publicity campaign was directed towards fending off the threat of nationalisation following the Labour Party's victory in the general election of 1945. Meanwhile, in an age of post-war austerity the quality of passenger train services remained abysmally low. Drained of resources and motivation the companies, apart from some orders for experimental diesel and gas-turbine locomotives, made do with worn out and obsolete equipment until nationalisation under the terms of the Transport Act of 1947.[35] From 1 January 1948 control of the railways and all the problems of providing their customers with adequate services passed to the British Transport Commission. Its creation marked the start of a new and arguably more tempestuous era in the relationship between the railway and its passengers.

Select Bibliography

Acworth, W. M. *The Railways of England,* 1900

Aldcroft, D. H. *British Railways in Transition. The Economic Problems of Britain's Railways Since 1914,* Macmillan, 1968

Aldcroft, D. H. *Studies in British Transport History,* David & Charles, 1974

Aldcroft, D. & Freeman, M. (eds) *Transport in the Industrial Revolution,* Manchester University Press, 1983

Alderman, G. *The Railway Interest,* Leicester University Press, 1973

Bagwell, P. S. *The Railway Clearing House in the British Economy 1844–1922,* 1968

Bagwell, P. S. *The Transport Revolution from 1770,* Batsford, 1974

Barker, T. C. & Robbins, M. *A History of London Transport: vols. 1 & 2,* Allen & Unwin, 1963 & 1974

Barman, C. *The Man Who Built London Transport: A Biography of Frank Pick,* David & Charles, 1979

Best, G. *Mid-Victorian Britain,* Panther, 1971

Bonavia, M. R. *Railway Policy Between the Wars,* Manchester University Press, 1981

Butterfield, P. 'Grouping, pooling and competition: the passenger policy of the London & North Eastern Railway, 1923–39', *Journal of Transport History,* 7, 2, 1986

Cain, P. J. 'Railway Combination and Government, 1900–1914', *Economic History Review,* XXV, 4, 1972

Cannadine, D. *Lords and Landlords: The Aristocracy and the Towns 1774–1967,* Leicester University Press, 1980

Cannadine, D. (ed) *Patricians, Power and Politics in Nineteenth Century Towns,* Leicester University Press, 1982

Carlson, R. E. *The Liverpool & Manchester Railway Project 1821–1831,* David & Charles, 1969

Carter, E. F. *Railways in Wartime,* Frederick Muller, 1964

Crompton, G. W. 'Efficient and Economical Working? The Performance of the Railway Companies 1923–33', *Business History,* XXVII 1985

Darwin, B. *War on the Line: the Story of the Southern Railway in War-Time,* 1946

Davies, W. J. K. *Light Railways,* Ian Allan, 1964

Donaghy, T. J. *Liverpool & Manchester Operations 1831–1845,* David & Charles, 1972

Dyos, H. J. 'Workmen's fares in South London 1860–1914', *Journal of Transport History,* 1,1, 1953

171

Select Bibliography

Dyos, H. J. 'Railways and Housing in Victorian London, *Journal of Transport History*, 2,1, 1955

Dyos, H. J. *Victorian Suburb: A Study of the Growth of Camberwell*, Leicester University Press, 1973

Dyos, H. J. & Aldcroft, D. H. *British Transport*, Leicester University Press, 1969

Findlay, G. *The Working and Management of an English Railway*, sixth edition, 1899

Foxwell, E. & Farrar, T. C. *Express Trains English and Foreign*, 1889

Gourvish, T. R. *Mark Huish and the London & North Western Railway*, (Leicester University Press, 1972)

Gourvish, T. R. 'The Performance of British Railway Management After 1860: The Railways of Watkin and Forbes', *Business History*, XX 1978

Gourvish, T. R. *Railways and The British Economy 1830–1914*, Macmillan, 1980

Grinling, C. H. *The History of the Great Northern Railway 1845–1922*, 1898

Hawke, G. R. *Railways and Economic Growth in England and Wales 1840–1870*, Clarendon Press, 1970

Head, F. *Stokers and Pokers*, 1894, David & Charles reprint, 1968

Jackson, A. A. *Semi-Detached London*, Allen & Unwin, 1973

Jackson, A. A. *London's Local Railways*, David & Charles, 1978

Jackson, A. A. *London's Termini*, David & Charles, 1984

Jenkinson, D. *Rails in the Fells*, Peco, 1980

Kellett, J. R. *Railways and Victorian Cities*, Routledge & Kegan Paul, 1979

Kichenside, G. *The Restaurant Car*, David & Charles, 1979

Liepmann, K. *The Journey to Work*, Kegan Paul, 1944

Lee, C. E. *Passenger Class Distinctions*, Railway Gazette, 1946

Legg, S. *The Railway Book*, 1958

McDermot, E. T. *History of the Great Western Railway, Vol 1*, revised edition, Ian Allan, 1972

Marshall, J. *The Lancashire & Yorkshire Railway, Vol 1*, David & Charles, 1969

Mather, F. C. 'The Railways, the Electric Telegraph and Public Order during the Chartist Period 1837–1848', *History*, XXXVIII, 1953

Mingay, G. E. (ed) *The Victorian Countryside*, Routledge & Kegan Paul, 1981

Nash, G. C. *The LMS at War*, 1946

Neele, G. P. *Railway Reminiscences*, 1904

Parris, H. *Government and the Railways in Nineteenth Century Britain*, Routledge & Kegan Paul, 1965

Parris, H. 'Northallerton to Hawes: A Study in Branch-Line History', *Journal of Transport History*, 2, 1955

Peacock, T. B. *Great Western Suburban Services*, Halstead, 1948

Perkin, H. J. *The Age of the Railway*, Panther, 1970

Select Bibliography

Pimlott, J. A. R. *The Englishman's Holiday,* Spiers, 1976

Pratt, E. A. *British Railways and the Great War Vols 1 & 2,* 1921

A Regional History of the Railways of Great Britain, David & Charles
    Vol 1, Thomas, D. St John *The West Country,* 1981
    Vol 2, White, H. P. *Southern England,* 1969
    Vol 5, Gordon, D. I. *The Eastern Counties,* 1968
    Vol 6, Thomas, J. *Scotland: the Lowlands and the Borders,* 1971
    Vol 7, Christiansen, R. *The West Midlands,* 1983
    Vol 8, Joy, D. *South and West Yorkshire,* 1975
    Vol 12, Barrie, D. S. M. *South Wales,* 1975

Richards, J. & MacKenzie, J. M. *The Railway Station: A Social History,* Oxford University Press, 1986

Robbins, M. *The Railway Age,* Penguin, 1965

Rolt, T. C. *Red for Danger,* Bodley Head, 1955

Schivelbusch, W. *The Railway Journey: Trains and Travel in the Nineteenth Century,* Basil Blackwell, 1980

Shackleton, J. T. *The Golden Age of the Railway Poster,* 1976

Simmons, J. *The Railways of Britain,* Macmillan, 1963

Simmons, J. *The Railway in England and Wales 1830–1914,* Vol 1, Leicester University Press, 1978

Simmons, J. 'Railways, hotels and tourism in Great Britain, 1839–1914, *Journal of Contemporary History,* 19, 2, 1984

Simmons, J. 'Suburban traffic at King's Cross 1852–1914', *Journal of Transport,* 6, 1, 1985

Simmons, J. *The Railway in Town and Country 1830–1914,* David & Charles, 1986

Storch, R. D. (ed) *Popular Culture and Custom in Nineteenth Century England,* Croom Helm, 1982

Thomas, D. St John, *The Country Railway,* David & Charles, 1976

Thompson, F. M. L. (ed) *The Rise of Suburbia,* Leicester University Press, 1982

Walton, J. K. 'Railways and Resort Development in North West England, 1830–1914', in Sigsworth, E. M. (ed) *Ports and Resorts in the Regions:* Hull College of Higher Education, 1980

Walton, J. K. 'The Demand for Working-Class Seaside Holidays in Victorian England', *Economic History Review,* XXXIV, 2, 1981

Walton, J. K. *The English Seaside Resort. A Social History 1750–1914,* Leicester University Press, 1983

Walvin, J. *Leisure and Society 1830–1950,* Longman, 1978

Wilson, R. B. *Go Great Western: A History of GWR Publicity,* David & Charles, 1970

Notes

Notes to Chapter 1 (*pages* 11–23)

1 J. S. Jeans, *History of the Stockton & Darlington Railway and a Record of its Results,* (1974), 79, 86

2 J. Francis, *A History of the English Railway. Its Social Relations and Revelations 1820–1945,* (1851), 96

3 P. S. Bagwell, *The Railway Clearing House in the British Economy 1842–1922,* (1968), 48. For important accounts of the early years of the L&MR see: R. E. Carlson, *The Liverpool & Manchester Railway Project 1821–1831* (1969); T. J. Donaghy, *Liverpool & Manchester Railway Operations 1831–1845,* (1969)

4 Cited in H. Pollins, *Britain's Railways: An Industrial History,* (1971), 58–9

5 These figures are drawn from T. R. Gourvish, *Railways and the British Economy 1830–1914,* (1980), 26; H. J. Dyos & D. H. Aldcroft, *British Transport,* (1969), 303

6 J. A. Chartres & G. L. Turnbull, 'Road Transport', in D. Aldcroft & M. Freeman, (eds), *Transport in the Industrial Revolution,* (1983), 69

7 E. W. Gilbert, *Brighton: Old Ocean's Bauble,* (1975), 116

8 J. Armstrong & P. S. Bagwell, 'Coastal Shipping', in Aldcroft & Freeman, (1983), 163–4

9 J. Lindsay, 'Passenger Traffic on British Canals: the Correspondence of William Houston 1830–1835', *Transport History,* 9, 3, 1978, 205; P. S. Bagwell, *The Transport Revolution,* (1974), 30

10 Chartres & Turnbull, (1983), 66

11 Bagwell, (1974), 55

12 *Royal Commission on Railways, Report, Parl. Papers (PP),* 1867, XXXVIII, 53

13 J. Simmons, *The Railway in England and Wales 1830–1914,* (1978), 271

14 Donaghy (1972), iii. For the aristocracy and the railway, see, F. M. L. Thompson, *English Landed Society in the Nineteenth Century,* (1963), 190 and passim

15 The first major study by a reputable body was published by the *Lancet* in 1862, see W. Schivelbusch, *The Railway Journey,* (1979), 118

16 A. B. Granville, *Spas of England and Principal Sea Bathing Places: The North,* (1841), 28

17 C. E. Lee, *Passenger Class Distinctions,* (1946), 9; Donaghy, (1972), 110–11

18 *Select Committee on Railways, Minutes of Evidence, PP*, 1839, X, q. 4924
19 *Ibid*, q. 5844; Lee, (1946), 16
20 *Railway News*, 10 February, 1883
21 *Select Committee on Railways, Report, PP*, 1839, X, vii; Gourvish, (1980), 26, for the commercial policies of the early companies.
22 G. R. Hawke, *Railways and Economic Growth in England and Wales 1840–1870*, (1970), 37–40
23 Lee, (1946), 21
24 *Ibid.*, 43; Simmons, (1978), 196
25 *Ibid.*, 198
26 Pecqueur, *(Economie Sociale)*, cited in Schivelbusch, (1979), 74–5
27 B. Disraeli, *Sybil; or, The Two Nations*, 1845 (Penguin edn), 136

Notes to Chapter 2 *(pages 24–44)*
 1 *Herapath's Railway and Commercial Journal*, 26 April 1845, 611
 2 H. Parris, *Government and the Railways in Nineteenth-Century Britain*, (1965), 18
 3 *Select Committee on Railway Acts Enactments, Second Report, PP*, 1846, XIV, ix
 4 A. Milward & S. B. Saul, *The Economic Development of Continental Europe*, (1973), 382, 422; T. Kemp, *Industrialisation in Nineteenth Century Europe*, (1969), 64–5
 5 F. C. Mather, 'The Railways, the Electric Telegraph and Public Order during the Chartist Period, 1837–48', *History*, xxxviii, (1953), 40–53
 6 *Report of the Commissioners appointed to inquire into the merits of the broad and narrow gauge, PP*, 1846, XVI, 6
 7 *Select Committee on Railways, Second Report, PP*, 1839, X, vii
 8 *Select Committee on Railway Companies' Amalgamation, Report, PP*, 1872, XIII, pt. 1, xxx
 9 P. S. Bagwell, *The Railway Clearing House in the British Economy 1842–1922*, (1968), especially chapter 10; Parris, (1965), 7; L. T. C. Rolt, *Red for Danger*, (1955), 24–5
10 *The Railway Traveller's Handy Book 1862*, (1971 ed), 81
11 Cited in S. Legg (ed), *The Railway Book*, (1952), 154–5
12 *The Railway Traveller's Handy Book*, 80
13 5 & 6 Vict. cap. 55, Sect. 6
14 Parris, (1965), 145; Rolt, (1955), 18–19; M. Robbins, *The Railway Age*, (1962), 97
15 31 & 32 Vict. cap. 119, Sect. 22
16 *Hansard*, House of Lords, CCXIV, 13 February 1873, 375; *Royal Commission on Railway Accidents, Report, PP*, 1877, XLVIII, 8
17 *Hansard*, House of Lords, CCXIV, 18 February 1873, 589
18 *Royal Commission on Railway Accidents, Report, PP*, 1877, XLVIII, 15
19 *Ibid.*, 21

20 *Railway News,* 19 April 1890, 782

21 T. R. Gourvish, *Railways and the British Economy 1830–1914,* (1980), 52

22 G. Alderman, *The Railway Interest,* (1973), 53–5

23 Rolt, (1955), 187–93; 52 & 53 Vict. cap. 57

24 P. W. Kingsford, *Victorian Railwaymen* (1970), 17–18

25 *Herapath's Railway Journal,* 19 September 1840, 717

26 H. A. Clegg, A. Fox & A. F. Thompson, *A History of British Trade Unions since 1889,* Vol. 1 1889–1910, (1964), 233–4

27 Although as J. Simmons has argued the railway inspectorate generally treated workers fairly, there was a tendency to identify the inspectorate with the companies and the 'establishment', see J. Simmons, *The Railway in England and Wales 1830–1914,* (1978), 236–7

28 7 & 8 Vict. cap. 85, Sect. 6, 9

29 C. E. Lee, *Passenger Class Distinctions,* (1946), 18

30 Simmons, (1978), 37–8

31 *Railway Traveller's Handy Book,* 49

32 Parris, (1965), 93–7

33 7 & 8 Vict. cap. 95, Sect. 8

34 Parris, (1965), 97, 143

35 Alderman, (1973), 82

36 26 & 27 Vict. cap. 33, Sect. 14

37 The railway companies' campaign and that of the Travelling Tax Abolition Committee are discussed by Alderman (1973), 83–94. See also G. J. Holyoake, *History of the Travelling Tax,* (1901), for a discussion from a different perspective.

38 H. J. Dyos, 'Railways and Housing in Victorian London', *Journal of Transport History,* 2, 1, (1955), 13

39 *Select Committee on Railway Companies' Amalgamation, Minutes of Evidence, PP,* 1872, XIII, especially the evidence of J. Raynor (Town Clerk of Liverpool) and W. B. Forwood, qs. 789, 1130

40 46 & 47 Vict. cap. 34, Sect. 2 (1)

41 *Ibid.,* Sect. 3

42 A memorial sent to Gladstone in July 1883 protesting against the provisions of the Passenger Duty Bill claimed to represent 'the railway shareholders of the Kingdom'. However the four main signatories were the representatives of Watkin's companies – the MSL, SER, ELR and Metropolitan. See *Railway News,* 4 August 1883, 187

43 D. H. Aldcroft, *British Railways in Transition,* (1968), 60. By this time nearly one-fifth of railway journeys were made on workmen's tickets; see K. K. Liepmann, *The Journey to Work,* (1944), 31

44 *Report of the Railway Department of the Board of Trade on Proposed Amalgamations of Railways, PP,* 1845, XXXIX, 1

45 *Select Committee on Railways, Third Report, PP,* 1844, XI, 2

46 E. Cleveland-Stevens, *English Railways Their Development and Their*

Relation to the State, (1915), 10

47 *Select Committee on Railways and Canals Amalgamations, First Report, PP,* 1846, XIII, 4

48 *Select Committee on Railway Companies' Amalgamation, Minutes of Evidence, PP,* 1872, XIII, pt. 1, qs. 4492, 4494, 5191

49 Aldcroft, (1968), 8

50 W. E. Simnet, *Railway Amalgamation in Great Britain,* (1923), 17

51 H. J. Dyos & D. H. Aldcroft, *British Transport,* (1969), 282–5, 290–3, for a survey of the economic effects of the First World War on the railways

52 Simnet, (1923), 24

53 *Select Committee on Railways, Third Report, PP,* 1844, XI, 6

54 Of the large numbers of railway directors in both Houses of Parliament the most important group – the 'efficient interest' – were those who were prepared to put railways before party. After 1868 the efficient interest in the Commons numbered 39. Thereafter, until 1906, the number only once fell below 32. See G. Alderman, *The Railway Interest,* (1973), 232–48. For the early development and organisation of the railway interest see P. S. Bagwell, 'The Railway Interest: Its Organisation and Influence', *Journal of Transport History,* 7, 2, (1965), 65

55 D. H. Aldcroft, 'The decontrol of shipping and railways after the First World War', *Journal of Transport History,* 5, (1961); S. M. H. Armitage, *The Politics of Decontrol of Industry: Britain and the United States,* (1969). Geddes had long advocated the amalgamation of railways into regional systems; see P. K. Cline, 'Eric Geddes and the "Experiment" with Businessmen in Government, 1915–22', in K. D. Brown (ed), *Essays in Anti-Labour History,* (1974), 97

56 Dyos & Aldcroft, (1969), 290–7, for a concise appraisal of the Act and its weaknesses

57 *Parl. Debates,* 5th Series, 142, 26 May 1921, 362

58 P. Butterfield, 'Grouping, pooling and competition. The passenger policy of the London & North Eastern Railway, 1923–39', *Journal of Transport History,* 7, 2, 1986, 23

59 Aldcroft, (1968), 46

Notes to Chapter 3 (*pages* 45–70)

1 C. L. Mowat, 'The Heyday of the British Railway System: Vanishing Evidence and the Historian's Task', *Journal of Transport History,* 1, 1, 1971, 1

2 P. Mathias, *The First Industrial Nation. An Economic History of Britain 1700–1914,* (1974), 284

3 H. Pollins, *Britain's Railways: An Industrial History,* (1971), 57

4 F. S. Williams, *Our Iron Roads,* Vol. 1, (1883), 63–4

5 P. S. Bagwell, *The Transport Revolution from 1770,* (1974), 107

6 H. J. Dyos & D. H. Aldcroft, *British Transport,* (1969), 129

7 Both examples are from F. M. L. Thompson, *English Landed Society in the Nineteenth Century*, (1963), 258–9

8 *Ibid.*, 260. For an important regional study of landowners' attitudes see, J. T. Ward, 'West Riding Landowners and the Railways', *Journal of Transport History*, 4, 4, 1960

9 J. Richards & J. M. MacKenzie, *The Railway Station A Social History*, (1986), 23–4

10 J. R. Kellett, *Railways and Victorian Cities*, (1979), 79

11 *Ibid.*, 290, 324–36

12 A. A. Jackson, *London's Termini*, (1972), 72–3, and J. Simmons, 'Suburban Traffic at King's Cross 1852–1914', *Journal of Transport History*, 6, 1, 1985, 71–8, for the difficulties of operating King's Cross station

13 Samuel Smiles, John Charles Rees & Edward Ryde, *Statement in Support of the Proposed London Bridge and Charing Cross Railway*, February 1858, Public Record Office (PRO), ZLIB 15/14/1

14 F. M. L. Thompson, 'Nineteenth-Century Horse Sense', *Economic History Review*, XXIX, (1976), 61

15 Richards & MacKenzie, (1986), 26–7, for a brief survey of the neglected history of railway hotels

16 *The Grand Junction, and Liverpool and Manchester Railway Companion*, (1837), 5–6

17 *Select Committee on Railway Acts Enactments, Second Report*, PP, 1846, XIV, xi

18 See *Bradshaw's Railway Companion*.

19 G. Findlay, *The Working and Management of an English Railway*, (1899), 318–9

20 G. R. Hawke, *Railways and Economic Growth in England and Wales 1840–1870*, (1970), 51

21 Cited in F. S. Williams, *Our Iron Roads*, Vol. 2, (1883), 391

22 E. T. MacDermot, *History of the Great Western Railway*, Vol. 1, 340–1

23 T. R. Gourvish, 'British Railway Management in the Nineteenth Century, with Special Reference to the Career of Captain Mark Huish, 1808–1867', (London Ph.D thesis, 1967), 159, 247–8

24 Railway Clearing House, General Managers Meeting, *Minutes*, 12 March 1867, PRO, RAIL 1081, 9, 717–18

25 *Ibid.*, 719

26 *Select Committee on Railways, Minutes of Evidence*, PP, 1839, X, evidence of Charles Buck, q. 4016

27 *Herapath's Railway Magazine and Commercial Journal*, 17 August 1839, 16

28 P. S. Bagwell, *The Railway Clearing House in the British Economy 1842–1922*, (1968), 49–50, 60

29 *Ibid.*, 61

30 M. R. Stones, 'Containers of Comfort', *Railway Magazine*, 131,

February 1985, 68–9

31 The first service between London and Bradford inaugurated in 1874 provided sleeping accommodation, although the carriages could be converted for day-time use. Pullmans were adopted by eight other companies: GNR, LBSC, LC&D, SER, Metropolitan, LSWR, Highland Railway and Caledonian

32 *Railway News,* 27 January 1883

33 Findlay, (1899), 319

34 The GWR entered a 99 year agreement with the Swindon Junction Hotel Co. to stop all its trains for at least ten minutes. The agreement remained in force until 1895 when the GWR bought the company out. 'Voyageur', 'Modern British Restaurant Car Services', *Railway Magazine,* XXXII, 1913, and G. Kichenside, *The Restaurant Car,* (1979), for the development of restaurant car services.

35 In 1868 the total daily express train mileage in Great Britain was 62,904, only 7 per cent of which was covered by trains without third-class accommodation. See E. Foxwell & T. C. Farrar, *Express Trains English and Foreign,* (1889), 66

36 E. Hobsbawm, *Worlds of Labour,* (1984), 200, for this argument in a wider context

37 *Railway News,* 2 November 1889. The companies were the Midland, LNWR, GWR and LBSC

38 Williams, Vol. 2, (1883), 389

39 *Railway News,* 27 January 1883, 164

40 W. Ashworth, *An Economic History of England 1870–1939,* (1960), 121

41 T. R. Gourvish, 'The Performance of British Railway Management After 1860: The Railways of Watkin and Forbes', *Business History,* XX, 1978, 189–99

42 Findlay, (1899), 316

43 Foxwell & Farrar, (1889), 68

44 '100-Mile Runs in 1913', *Railway Magazine,* XXXIII, 1913, 244–6; J. Simmons, *The Railway in England and Wales 1830–1914,* (1978), Appendix 1, 271

45 H. J. Dyos & D. H. Aldcroft, *British Transport,* (1969), 284

46 'Voyageur', 'British Winter Express Train Services 1921–22', *Railway Magazine,* XLVIII, 1921, 389

47 The train ran over the lines of the North British, North Eastern, Great Central and Great Western; see *Modern Transport,* 8 October 1921

48 *Memorandum to the Minister of Transport in Reply to the Memorandum upon the position of the Main Line Companies in relation to Road Transport Competition,* Conference of Motor Organisations, March 1932, 4

49 Average receipts per passenger mile fell from 0.86d in 1921 to 0.67d in 1938; see Bagwell, (1974), 253

50 P. Butterfield, 'Grouping, pooling and competition: the passenger

policy of the London & North Eastern Railway, 1923–39', *Journal of Transport History*, 7, 2, 1986, 29

51 J. C. Chambers, 'Interavailable Ticket Facilties', *Modern Transport*, 18 February 1939

52 Butterfield, (1986), 26

53 M. R. Bonavia, *The Four Great Railways*, (1980), 111

Notes to Chapter 4 (*pages 71–88*)

1 A. Frater, *StoppingTrain Britain*, (1983); D. St John Thomas & P. Whitehouse, *Great Days of the Country Railway*, (1986), for two examples of this voluminous literature

2 D. St John Thomas, *The Country Railway*, (1976), 44

3 J. Simmons, *The Railway in Town and Country 1830–1914*, (1986), 334

4 *Herapath's Journal and Railway Magazine*, 8 February 1845, 146–7

5 Simmons, (1986), 324–5

6 Sir George Head, *A Home Tour Through the Manufacturing Districts of England in the Summer of 1835*, 427

7 E. Griffith, *The Bishops Castle Railway*, (1969)

8 W. J. K. Davies, *Light Railways*, (1964), 54, 66

9 J. Scott Morgan, *The Colonel Stephens Railways*, (1978); and P. Shaw, 'Holman Fred Stephens – light railway engineer extraordinary', *Railway World*, 37, January 1976, 34–6

10 H. W. Parris, 'Northallerton to Hawes: A Study in Branch-Line History', *Journal of Transport History*, II, 1955–6, 246

11 H. Pollins, 'Railway Contractors and the Finance of Railway Development in Britain', *Journal of Transport History*, III, 1957–8

12 *Select Committee on Railway Acts Enactments, Minutes of Evidence, PP*, 1846, XIV, evidence of S. M. Peto, qs. 3431, 3436

13 D. H. Aldcroft, *British Railways in Transition*, (1968), 9–10

14 M. V. Searle, *Lost Lines*, (1982), 128–9; K. Jones, 'Buckinghamshire byway: origin rise and fall of the rural Wotton tramway', *Railway Magazine*, 119, March 1973, 127–9

15 Hawke argues that overall the savings to the economy of England and Wales contributed by railway services (passenger and freight) in 1865 amounted to 10 per cent of net national income. See G. R. Hawke, *Railways and Economic Growth in England and Wales 1840–1870*, (1970), passim

16 *Ibid.*, 191–4

17 D. W. Howell, 'The Impact of Railways on Agricultural Development in Nineteenth-Century Wales', *Welsh History Review*, 7, 1974–5, 60–2

18 A. Redford, *Labour Migration in England 1800–1850*, (1976), 122; D. Brooke, *The Railway Navvy*, (1983), especially ch. 1.

19 *Royal Commission on the Housing of the Working Classes, Minutes of Evidence, PP*, 1884–85, XXX, q. 10,615

20 M. Anderson, *Family Structure in Nineteenth-Century Lancashire,* (1971)

21 W. Hasbach, *A History of the English Agricultural Labourer,* (1908), 345

22 Cited in J. D. Chambers & G. E. Mingay, *The Agricultural Revolution 1750–1880,* (1966), 188

23 Even in London it was difficult for workers to find out what work was available in neighbouring districts. See E. J. Hobsbawm, *Worlds of Labour,* (1984), ch. 8

24 E. L. Taplin, *Liverpool Dockers and Seamen 1870–1890,* (1974), 39

25 R. Lawton, 'David Brindley's Liverpool', *Transactions of the Historic Society of Lancashire and Cheshire,* 125, 1974, 157

26 Redford, (1976), 188. See also A. Constant, 'The Geographical Background of Inter-Village Population Movements in Northamptonshire and Huntingdonshire 1754–1943', *Geography,* XXXIII, 1948, 78–88

27 D. Jenkinson, *Rails in the Fells,* (1980), 84–5, 94

28 Simmons, (1986), 16–19 and ch. 9

29 P. S. Bagwell, 'The Decline of Rural Isolation', in G. E. Mingay, *The Victorian Countryside,* (1981), 40

30 A. Everitt, 'Town and Country in Victorian Leicestershire: The Role of the Village Carrier', in Everitt (ed), *Perspectives in English Urban History,* (1973), 217–19. For the earlier development of carrier services see, J. A. Chartres & G. L. Turnbull, 'Road Transport', in D. H. Aldcroft & M. Freeman, *Transport in the Industrial Revolution,* (1983)

31 Coastwise trade carried by steamships remained an exception. However, the role of coastal shipping was modified by the railways. For some shipping concerns survival came by providing a complementary service to the railways or, in some cases, acting in collusion with them on pricing and cargoes. See C. H. Lee, 'Some Aspects of the Coastal Shipping Trade: The Aberdeen Steam Navigation Company, 1835–80', *Journal of Transport History,* II, 2, 1975

32 Jenkinson, (1980), 95–102

33 Simmons, (1986), 326

34 P. Horn, *The Rural World 1780–1850,* (1980), 242

35 Redford, (1976), 190

36 M. Hillman & A. Whalley, *The Social Consequence of Rail Closures,* Policy Studies Institute, (1980), 17–26

37 Parris, (1955–6)

38 Jenkinson, (1980), 100

39 Simmons, (1986), 314–5

40 Aldcroft, (1968), 21–2

41 J. Simmons, *The Railway in England and Wales 1830–1914,* (1978), 111

42 Davies, (1964), 59

43 Aldcroft, (1968), 64–5; Dyos & Aldcroft, *British Transport*, (1969), 319

44 P. Butterfield, 'Grouping, pooling and competition: the passenger policy of the London & North Eastern Railway, 1923–39', *Journal of Transport History*, 7, 2, 1986, 32–4

45 C. R. Dalby, 'Some aspects of special traffic working by passenger train services with special reference to excursion traffic', Typescript Paper, (1938), 19–20

46 Cited in *Modern Transport*, 21 January 1939, 12

47 Parris, (1955–6), 235

Notes to Chapter 5 (*pages 89–112*)

 1 *Herapath's Railway Journal*, 13 September 1845, 1627

 2 J. R. Kellett, *Railways and Victorian Cities*, (1979), 365

 3 See T. C. Barker & M. Robbins, *A History of London Transport*, Vol. 1, (1963); E. Course, *London Railways*, (1962); and H. P. White, *A Regional History of the Railways of Great Britain: Southern England*, (1961), and *Greater London*, (1963)

 4 A rectangular area bounded by the present-day streets of the Marylebone and Euston Roads, the City Road, Finsbury Square, Bishopsgate Street, London Bridge, Borough High Street, Vauxhall Bridge, Grosvenor Gardens and Park Lane. See J. Simmons, *The Railway in England and Wales 1830–1914*, (1978), 116

 5 The fear that smoke and fume-laden tunnels would deter passengers led the line's engineer, John Fowler, to experiment with a fireless locomotive known as 'Fowler's Ghost'. See "Steamologist", 'Facts and Fables of Fowler's Ghost', *Railway World*, 35, January & February 1974; M. Seymour, 'The Ghost Walks Again', *Ibid.*, 35, October 1974

 6 T. B. Peacock, *Great Western Suburban Services*, (1948), 19; Barker & Robbins, (1963), 129; E. G. Barnes, 'Midland Jostles to the City', *Railway Magazine*, 118, September 1972, 460

 7 Browning Hall Conference, *Report of Sub-Committee on Housing and Locomotion in London 1902–1907*, April 1907, 16

 8 J. W. Graham, *The Line Beneath the Liners*, (1983), 34; J. Marshall, *The Lancashire & Yorkshire Railway*, (1970), 157

 9 M. Blakemore, 'Metropolis to Metroland', *Railway Magazine*, 126, October 1980; G. Holt, *A Regional History of the Railways of Great Britain: The North West*, (1978)

10 R. Christiansen, *A Regional History of the Railways of Britain: The West Midlands*, (1983), 40, 78

11 Kellett, (1979), 354–5

12 J. Foster, *Class Struggle and the Industrial Revolution*, (1974), 182

13 Kellett, (1979), 354–76

14 This paragraph is based on J. M. Rawcliffe, 'Bromley: Kentish market town to London suburb', in F. M. L. Thompson (ed), *The Rise of*

Suburbia, (1982), 28–91

15 The branch to Hayes and suburban growth in the district is discussed in A. A. Jackson, *London's Local Railways,* (1978), 266–271

16 Rawcliffe, (1982), 53. Bexley was another community where suburban growth did not follow immediately after the arrival of the railway. For this and other examples see the essays in Thompson (1982)

17 *Southport Visiter,* 28 July 1849

18 J. Liddle, 'Estate management and land reform politics: the Hesketh and Scarisbrick families and the making of Southport, 1842–1914', in D. Cannadine (ed), *Patricians Power and Politics in Nineteenth-Century Towns,* (1982), 144 and passim

19 D. Cannadine, *Lords and Landlords. The Aristocracy and the Towns, 1774–1967,* (1980), 18

20 Thompson, (1982), 18

21 Browning Hall Conference, *Report,* 1907, 301

22 H. J. Dyos, *Victorian Suburb,* (1973), 23

23 C. Booth, 'Improved Means of Locomotion as a Cure for the Housing Difficulties of London', *Browning Hall Conference,* 1901, 15

24 C. Dickens, *Dombey and Son,* (1848, Penguin ed), 121

25 C. E. Lee, *Passenger Class Distinctions,* (1946), 51–3

26 *Ibid.,* 50

27 *Railway News,* 21 June 1890, 1229

28 *Royal Commission on the Housing of the Working Classes, Minutes of Evidence, PP,* 1884–85, XXX, evidence of H. G. Calcraft, q. 9,979

29 *Railway News,* 21 June 1890, 1229

30 *Royal Commission on the Housing of the Working Classes, First Report, PP,* 1884–85, XXX, 51

31 Browning Hall Conference, *Report of Sub-Committee on Locomotion,* 1902, 6

32 Lee, (1946), 57

33 H. J. Dyos, 'Workmen's fares in South London, 1860–1914', *Journal of Transport History,* 1, 1, 1953, 12

34 Kellett, (1979), 93–4

35 Dyos, (1953), 6

36 Cited in Booth, 1901, 2

37 *Ibid.,* 6

38 Kellett, (1979), 410

39 *Royal Commission on the Housing of the Working Classes, First Report, PP,* 1884–85, XXX, 49

40 C. H. Grinling, *The History of the Great Northern Railway, 1845–1922,* (1966 ed), 349

41 *Royal Commission on the Housing of the Working Classes, Minutes of Evidence, PP,* 1884–85, XXX, evidence of William Birt, q. 10,209

42 Cited in Lee, (1946), 27

43 Kellett, (1979), 388–400, for this argument

44 *Royal Commission on the Housing of the Working Classes, First Report, PP,* 1884–85, XXX, 50
45 W. M. Acworth, *The Railways of England,* (1900), 426
46 Dyos, (1953), 16
47 *Ibid.,* 18
48 A. S. Wohl, 'The Housing of the Working Classes in London 1815–1914', in S. D. Chapman (ed), *The History of Working Class Housing,* (1971), 17
49 Kellett, (1979), 379
50 Wohl, (1971), 36
51 H. J. Perkin, *The Age of the Automobile,* (1976), 149
52 A. A. Jackson, *Semi-Detached London,* (1973), 294–6, for the transport problems facing Becontree in these years
53 Dyos & Aldcroft, *British Transport,* (1969), 305; D. H. Aldcroft, *British Transport Since 1914,* (1975), 37–8
54 Barker & Robbins, (1963), 247–52
55 R. H. Selbie, 'Railways and Land Development', in *Modern Transport,* 11 June 1921
56 Dendy Marshall, *History of the Southern Railway,* (1963), 401
57 *Royal Commission on Transport, Final Report,* Cmd 3751, 1931, 39
58 C. J. Allen, *The Great Eastern Railway,* (1975), 184–9
59 *Royal Commission on Transport, Final Report,* Cmd 3751, 1931, 39
60 Dyos & Aldcroft, (1969), 310

Notes to Chapter 6 (*pages* 113–135)

1 D. Cannadine, 'The Present and the Past in the English Industrial Revolution 1880–1980', *Past & Present,* 103, 1984, for a most informative survey of writing on the Industrial Revolution. See also R. Cameron, 'A New View of European Industrialisation', *Economic History Review,* XXXVIII, 1, 1985, for a reassessment of industrialisation in the European context.
2 E. P. Thompson, 'Time, Work-Discipline, and Industrial Capitalism', *Past & Present,* 38, 1967; and E. Hopkins, 'Working Hours and Conditions during the Industrial Revolution: a Re-appraisal', *Economic History Review,* XXXV, 1, 1982, for two contrasting interpretations of the impact of industrialisation on work and leisure
3 J. K. Walton & R. Poole, 'The Lancashire Wakes in the Nineteenth Century', in R. D. Storch (ed), *Popular Culture and Custom in Nineteenth Century-England,* (1982), 102
4 *Ibid.* See also R. Malcomson, *Popular Recreations in English Society 1700–1850,* (1973)
5 Cited in J. A. R. Pimlott, *The Englishman's Holiday,* (1976), 95
6 *Herapath's Journal and Railway Magazine,* 12 October 1850
7 J. Pudney, *The Thomas Cook Story,* (1953), 53
8 P. J. Gooderson, 'Railway Construction in Mid-Nineteenth Century North Lancashire. A Study Based on the Diary of James Stelfox

1855–70', *Transactions of the Historic Society of Lancashire &
Cheshire*, 122, 1970, 147

9 J. K. Walton, *The English Seaside Resort. A Social History
1750–1914*, (1983), 28

10 Cited in Pimlott, (1976), 94

11 Bass, Ratcliff & Gretton, *Excursion to Great Yarmouth*, 1893

12 H. J. Perkin, *Age of the Railway*, (1970), 99; P. S. Bagwell, *The
Railway Clearing House in the British Economy 1842–1922*, (1968),
56–7

13 Cited in *Railway News*, 3 August 1889

14 Household Tracts for the People, *Sunday Excursions*, (1863), 29–32

15 D. A. Reid, 'The Decline of Saint Monday 1766–1876', *Past &
Present*, 71, 1976, 82

16 *Herapath's Journal*, 28 September 1850

17 Walton, (1983), 194–5

18 M. Huggins, 'Social Tone and Resort Development in North-East
England', *Northern History*, XX, 1984, 202

19 A. Gray, 'Crime on the Railways', *Railway Magazine*, November
1986, 703

20 J. Walvin, *Leisure and Society*, (1978)

21 J. Richards & J. M. MacKenzie, *The Railway Station. A Social
History*, (1986), 178

22 E. W. Gilbert, *Brighton: Old Ocean's Bauble*, (1975), 195

23 G. Best, *Mid-Victorian Britain 1851–1871*, (1973), 222–4

24 Walton, (1983), 197

25 G. Stedman Jones, 'Class Expression Versus Social Control: A
Critique of Recent Trends in the Social History of Leisure', *History
Workshop Journal*, 4 1977

26 J. Armstrong & P. S. Bagwell, 'Coastal Shipping' in D. H. Aldcroft &
M. Freeman, *Transport in the Industrial Revolution*, (1983), 162

27 J. K. Walton, 'The Demand for Working-Class Seaside Holidays in
Victorian England', *Economic History Review*, XXXIV, 2, 1981,
252–3

28 J. Simmons, *The Railway in Town and Country 1830–1914*, (1986),
255–9

29 J. K. Walton, 'Railways and Resort Development in North West
England, 1830–1914', in E. M. Sigsworth (ed), *Ports and Resorts in
the Regions*, (1980), 124–5

30 Walton, (1981), 253–6

31 Huggins, (1984), 197

32 H. J. Perkin, 'The Social Tone of Victorian Resorts in the North West',
Northern History, XI, 1976, 180–94

33 W. Wordsworth, *Guide to the Lakes*, (5th ed, 1835), 155

34 L. A. Williams, *Road Transport in Cumbria in the Nineteenth
Century*, (1975), 121. For further discussion of seasonal variations
and the breakdown of traffic between classes, see J. K. Walton, 'The

Windermere tourist trade in the age of the railway, 1847–1912', in O. M. Westall (ed), *Windermere in the Nineteenth Century*, (1976), 23

35 *Railway News,* 10 March 1883
36 *Railway Magazine,* XXXII, 1913
37 G. Findlay, *The Working and Management of an English Railway,* (1899), 358–60
38 W. McGowan Gradon, *A History of the Cockermouth, Keswick and Penrith Railway,* (1948), 10
39 E. A. Pratt, *British Railways and the Great War,* Vol. 1, (1921), 131
40 J. A. R. Pimlott, (1976), 221
41 C. D. Buchanan, *Mixed Blessing The Motor in Britain,* (1958), 67

Notes to Chapter 7 *(pages 136–154)*

1 T. J. Donaghy, *Liverpool & Manchester Railway Operations 1831–1845,* (1972), 114
2 P. S. Bagwell, *The Railway Clearing House in the British Economy 1842–1922,* (1969), 56
3 Railway Clearing House, General Managers' Meeting, *Mintues,* 22 May 1851, PRO RAIL1081/8, Vol. 1, 1849–60
4 *Ibid.,* 13 September 1854, 12 February 1857, 12 March 1867, PRO RAIL 1081/8/9, Vols. 1 & 2, 1849–60, 1861–68
5 Railway Clearing House, Superintendents' Meetings, *Minutes,* 7 April 1857, PRO RAIL 1081/43/44, 1850–60, 1861–66
6 *Ibid.,* special meeting of Superintendents at Scarborough on 4–5 March 1875, adjourned to 18–20 March, PRO RAIL 1081/47, 1875–78
7 *Ibid.,* 7–8 March 1877
8 C. R. Dalby, 'Some aspects of special traffic working by passenger train services with special reference to excursion traffic', typescript paper, 1938, 12
9 H. J. Dyos & D. H. Aldcroft, *British Transport,* (1969), 315
10 O. S. Nock, *The Great Western Railway in the Twentieth Century,* (1971), 128
11 M. Robbins, *The Railway Age,* (1965), 146–7. See also E. F. Carter, *Railways in Wartime,* (1964)
12 T. C. Mather, 'The Railways, Electric Telegraph and Public Order during the Chartist Period, 1837–48', *History,* XXXVIII, (1953), 45
13 Robbins, (1965), 141
14 G. Findlay, LNWR, cited in *Railway News,* 28 June 1890, 1303
15 E. A. Pratt, *British Railways and the Great War,* Vol. 1, (1921), 40
16 *Ibid.,* 113
17 A. Jackson, *London's Termini,* (1985), 252, 288
18 Pratt, (1921), 124–5
19 The most serious delay occurred early in 1918 when deep snow trapped the special at Scotscalder near Thurso. See H. A. Vallance, *The*

Highland Railway, (1972), 110
20 Pratt, (1921), 221–2
21 G. C. Nash, The LMS at War, (1946), 7
22 J. Richards & J. M. MacKenzie, *The Railway Station. A Social History,* (1986), 277
23 P. S. Bagwell, *The Transport Revolution from 1770,* (1974), 299
24 Hamilton Ellis, *London Midland & Scottish,* (1970), 181
25 D. H. Aldcroft, *British Railways in Transition,* (1968), 98–9
26 Hamilton Ellis, *British Railway History 1877–1947,* (1959), 372
27 *Ibid.,* 377
28 H. Gasson, *Firing Days,* (1973), 85
29 E. T. MacDermot, *History of the Great Western Railway,* Vol. 1, (1972), 350
30 Hamilton Ellis, *Royal Trains,* (1975), 8
31 J. Simmons, 'Railways, Hotels and Tourism in Great Britain 1839–1914', *Journal of Contemporary History,* 19, (1984), 211
32 G. P. Neele, *Railway Reminiscences,* (1904), 454
33 GNR, 'Her Majesty's Journey to Scotland', handbill of instructions to staff, (nd), J. Johnson Collection, Bodleian Library, Box 5
34 Neele, (1904), 504

Notes to Chapter 8 (*pages* 155–70)

1 T. R. Nevett, *Advertising in Britain. A History,* (1982), 60. See also J. T. Shackleton, *The Golden Age of the Railway Poster,* (1977)
2 H. J. Jewell, 'The Publicity Department', *Jubilee of the Railway News,* (1914), 213
3 *Ibid.*
4 R. Burdett Wilson, *Go Great Western. A History of GWR Publicity,* (1970), 22
5 J. Simmons, 'Railways, Hotels and Tourism in Great Britain 1839–1914', *Journal of Contemporary History,* 19 (1984), 206
6 *Ibid.,* 205–6
7 *Ibid.,* 210
8 G. P. Neele, *Railway Reminiscences,* (1904), 414
9 *Railway Magazine,* IV 1899, 562–8
10 LNWR, *Programme of Two Monthly Tickets,* 1877, R. B. Wilson Collection, Bodleian Library, Misc. Box
11 Jewell, (1914)
12 Wilson, (1970), 24–5
13 C. Barman, *The Man Who Built London Transport. A Biography of Frank Pick,* (1979), 26
14 *Ibid.,* 33
15 Wilson, (1970), 43
16 Barman, (1979), 26
17 *Railway Service Journal,* March 1930, 85
18 Wilson, (1970), 73–4

19 See, J. Johnson Collection, (Railways), Bodleian Library, which contains a mass of printed publicity material of this kind

20 Metropolitan and London & North Eastern Railways, *Country Walks in Metroland*, 3, J. Johnson Collection, Box 24

21 *Ibid.*

22 Wilson, (1970), 45

23 A. Davies (LMS), 'Salesmanship and the Railway', paper presented to the Railway Students' Association, 27 April 1939, 14

24 *Modern Transport*, 22 April 1939, 13

25 Wilson, (1970), 136

26 *Railway Service Journal*, March 1930, 85

27 *Ibid.*, September 1931, 361

28 Davies, (1939), 6

29 *Ibid.*, 9

30 P. Butterfield, 'Grouping, pooling and competition: the passenger policy of the London & North Eastern Railway, 1923–39', *Journal of Transport History*, 7, 2, 1986, 42

31 *Ibid.* See also M. R. Bonavia, *Twilight of British Rail*, (1985) for a comparison of railway services in the late 1930s with those of the 1980s

32 T. C. Barker & C. I. Savage, *An Economic History of Transport in Britain*, (1975), 158; H. Pollins, *Britain's Railways* (1971), 159; D. H. Aldcroft, *British Railways in Transition*, (1968), 67

33 G. W. Crompton, ' "Efficient and Economical Working"? The Performance of the Railway Companies 1923–33', *Business History*, XXVII, 2, 1985, 235. See also M. R. Bonavia, *Railway Policy Between the Wars*, (1981), for a defence of railway management during this period

34 *Royal Commission on Transport, Final Report*, Cmd 3751, 1931

35 Though see the GWR's 'valedictory gesture' *Next Station*, (1947) later reprinted as C. Barman, *The Great Western Railway's Last Look Forward*, (1972)

Acknowledgements

In writing this book I have accumulated a debt to several people. I owe the idea for a study of the relationship between the railway and its passengers to David St John Thomas. The first draft of the book was read and commented upon by Professor Philip Bagwell. I am most grateful for his advice and suggestions and also those of Dr John Walton. Any remaining deficiencies are due to the author. Finally, my daughter has been a constant source of inspiration because of her enthusiasm for everything to do with railways, while my wife has provided practical help and support at every stage of the book's evolution. Without her it would not have been possible.

Index

Index